COOL CAREERS WITHOUT COLLEGE FOR PEOPLE WHO CAN BUILD THINGS

NEW

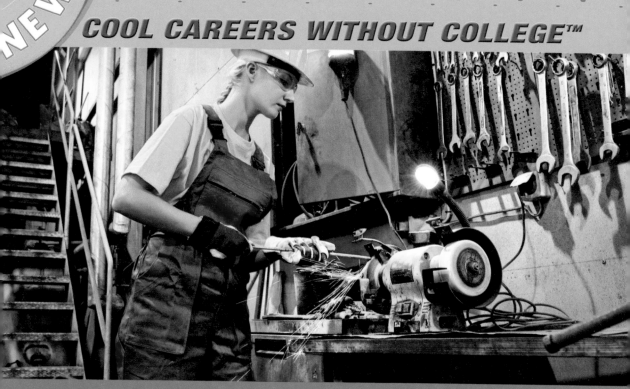

COOL CAREERS WITHOUT COLLEGE
FOR PEOPLE WHO CAN
BUILD THINGS

HEATHER MOORE NIVER

ROSEN
PUBLISHING®

New York

Published in 2014 by The Rosen Publishing Group, Inc.
29 East 21st Street, New York, NY 10010

First Edition

Library of Congress Cataloging-in-Publication Data

Niver, Heather Moore.
Cool careers without college for people who can build things/Heather Moore Niver. — First edition.
    pages cm. — (New cool careers without college)
Audience: Grades 7–12.
Includes bibliographical references and index.
ISBN 978-1-4777-1824-7
1. Engineering—Juvenile literature. 2. Manufacturing industries—Juvenile literature. 3. Decorative arts—Juvenile literature. I. Title.
TA149.N58 2014
602.3—dc23

3 1350 00336 2433

2013011260

Manufactured in the United States of America

CPSIA Compliance Information: Batch #W14YA: For further information, contact Rosen Publishing, New York, New York, at 1-800-237-9932.

A portion of the material in this book has been derived from *Cool Careers Without College for People Who Love to Build Things* by Joy Paige.

CONTENTS

INTRODUCTION

Everyone finds it a challenge to figure out what he or she wants to do to make a living. Sometimes going to college helps expose people to new ideas and career paths, but a secondary education isn't for everyone. Young people may be especially intimidated by the idea of picking a career they may follow for the rest of their lives. Older workers may want to change to a new career later in life without spending the time and money needed to go to college.

But just because university life isn't part of someone's life plan doesn't mean they're stuck trudging to a loathsome job every morning. So how does one start figuring out what kind of job he or she would enjoy doing? Most people start out by thinking about what they like to do. Hobbies such as working outside in the garden, sewing clothes, working with wood, or fixing cars are all good clues to figuring out what career would be a good fit for them.

Most of us spend our free time doing what we enjoy. Some people start to get interested in woodworking when they take a shop class or work with a family member on a house or other project. Others love planting seeds, watching them grow into plants and flowers, and creating beautiful flower

One way people decide on a career path is by thinking about what they enjoy doing. People who look forward to working with their hands, for example, might be happy working as carpenters.

gardens or more useful vegetable gardens. Either way, anyone reading this probably likes to build and create things. Even readers who are just learning about construction work, for example, may find that the other professions explored here are extremely tempting, too.

People who want to build things create more than just houses and buildings, of course. Construction workers build houses, but they also construct bridges, roads, and tunnels. Plumbers put in the pipes and fixtures that move water and other substances through buildings. Gardeners fill all kinds of spaces with beautiful plants, flowers, trees, and vegetables. Gems and stones become gorgeous rings, necklaces, and bracelets in the hands of jewelers. The shoes that protect our feet and look so good are made and repaired by shoemakers, while tailors and dressmakers work with fabric, thread, and other materials to make the clothing we wear every day. Sculptors work with everything from wood and stones to plastic and metal to create original, three-dimensional art. These are just a few building careers readers can explore.

With this resource, readers can learn about a variety of jobs available for people who like to create and build things. Visit the Bureau of Labor Statistics Web site for the most up-to-date information about average salaries. Not all of these careers are a cinch to obtain, but with some hard work and determination, almost anyone can find himself or herself a satisfying job.

CHAPTER 1

WORKING AS A TOOL AND DIE MAKER

Any device or implement made to complete a specific task can be considered a tool. Dies are metal forms that are also made to perform a particular task, such as cutting or molding metal or plastic into a specific shape, such as a car fender. Tools and dies make it possible for machines to accurately manufacture a product. Most products are made with tools and dies.

Tool and die makers create these tools from beginning to end. The manufacturing process depends on tools and dies because machines need proper parts to make merchandise from complex cell phones to simple shampoo bottles.

WHAT A TOOL AND DIE MAKER DOES

Tool and die makers set up and operate all kinds of machines that use computers to create metal parts, instruments, and tools that need to be an exact shape and size. Tool and die makers refer to blueprints, plans, drawings, or instructions to get an idea of what they are making. Then they must figure

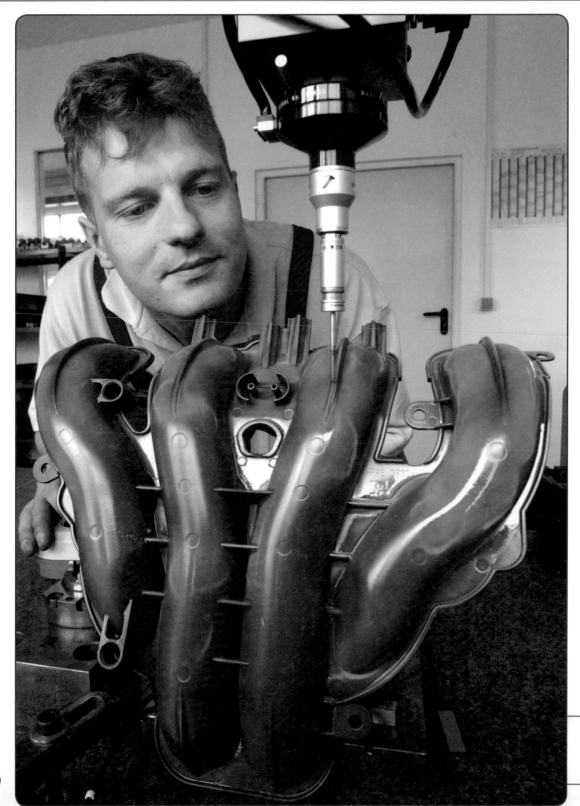

out how to make the tool or die. They draw up their own plan for how they want to make the product. The process of making a tool or die requires accuracy, so makers must concentrate, be methodical, and be determined.

To make their tools and dies, workers cut, form, or make a mold to construct the parts that will be combined as a completed product. When the pieces are ready, workers put them all together to form the finished tool or die. They may polish or grind the metal surface to make it smooth. Finally, workers must verify that their tool or die matches the original descriptions or plans. They check their product to make sure that it works properly.

Tool and die makers should know all about different kinds of metals, so they can decide on the best type to use for each job. To cut the metal, they may need to know how to use other machines, such as drills or grinders.

Computers help tool and die makers be more productive. Tool and die builders increasingly rely on computer-aided design (CAD) software to make their products. The CAD software helps calculate measurements and produce accurate drawings of the tool and die parts, which helps plan how to make them quickly and accurately.

A tool and die maker must be extremely skilled, have good judgment, and be precise. Whether workers generate both tools and dies or specialize in one or the other, their job works the same way and the skills are alike.

Tools and dies must follow exact measurements. After a tool or die is made, workers sometimes use computers to test it to make sure that the tool or die works correctly.

Because tool and die work requires specific skills, some training is usually required. This can occur on the job, through an apprenticeship program, or at a technical school.

TRAINING

Tool and die makers are highly skilled. Though a college education is unnecessary to become a tool or die maker, learning the trade takes four or five years of training. A formal apprenticeship program—which combines on-the-job training with classroom instruction—is an excellent way to gain experience. Few such programs exist, but one can also build skills through informal on-the-job training or classroom instruction at a vocational or technical school.

MACHINISTS, WELDERS, AND MORE

The skills of a tool and die maker can earn workers employment in other occupations that may interest them, too. Machinists work with machines, such as lathes, milling machines, and grinders, to produce metal parts to be used in products that range from bolts to antilock brakes. Much like tool and die makers, they work with machines to create a finished product.

A welder makes his or her living welding, in which heat is used to join pieces of metal. Welders work in industries from car racing to manufacturing. They may weld beams or pipes together for construction jobs. They may also weld parts together for bridge work. Cutters, solderers, and braziers also work with welding to join metal parts, fill holes and seams, and more, usually using handheld welding machines.

Metal and plastic machine workers assemble and run machines that cut, shape, and form plastic and metal materials or parts. Factory equipment and other industrial machinery, including conveying systems, production machinery, and packaging equipment, needs repair and general maintenance. Industrial machinery mechanics and maintenance workers are responsible for the care and repair of these machines and equipment. Machines in factories, power plants, and construction plants are set up, taken apart, fixed, reassembled, and moved by workers called millwrights.

According to the Bureau of Labor Statistics, any of these career paths require a high school diploma or its equivalent to get started. So anyone curious about working with machines, plastic, or metal should check out some of these careers.

By learning the steps involved in making tools and dies, one learns to operate the machines that help make them and learns how to read blueprints and plans. Good math skills are essential, as are good eyesight, excellent problem-solving abilities, and computer skills.

THE GOOD, THE BAD, AND THE UGLY

Skilled tool and die makers are rare these days. Although the work itself isn't dangerous, workers must be wary of pieces of metal unexpectedly flying through the air and loud machines. Most workers wear safety goggles and earplugs, and machines have protective gear to ensure their safety.

Tool and die makers often work in machine shops, on factory floors, and in tool rooms. These areas tend to be clean and well lit. Also, the rooms are kept cool to prevent the machines from overheating.

Over the past few years, manufacturers have increased production in the United States and are having trouble finding skilled tool and die workers. Although machines can make basic parts, workers need to form and put the tool and die together. Also, the skills that are obtained through training can be used throughout this industry and in other industries, such as making machinery used in aircrafts and automobiles.

FOR MORE INFORMATION

ORGANIZATIONS

Fabricators & Manufacturers Association, International (FMA)
833 Featherstone Road
Rockford, IL 61107
(815) 399-8700
Web site: http://www.fmanet.org
This professional organization boasts more than 2,300 individual and company members who work to improve the metal forming and fabricating industry.

National Tooling and Machining Association
1357 Rockside Road
Cleveland, OH 44134
(800) 248-6862
Web site: http://www.ntma.org
This organization of two thousand members was founded in 1943. It promotes apprenticeships programs and provides managerial workshops to those in the tooling and machining industry.

Tooling and Manufacturing Association
1177 South Dee Road
Park Ridge, IL 60068

(847) 825-1120

Web site: http://www.tmanet.com

The Tooling and Manufacturing Association is a nonprofit organization that exists to help people and companies in the tooling and manufacturing industries. The organization also offers courses and training programs.

WEB SITES

Due to the changing nature of Internet links, Rosen Publishing has developed an online list of Web sites related to the subject of this book. This site is updated regularly. Please use this link to access the list:

http://www.rosenlinks.com/CCWC/Build

BOOKS

Jeffus, Larry. *Welding: Principles and Applications*. 7th ed. Clifton Park, NY: Delmar Publishing, 2011.

Anyone interested in tool and die work will want to learn about welding basics. This book is useful to students and more advanced welders alike. It includes theories, safety guidelines, and basic welding techniques.

Lipton, Tom. *Metalworking Sink or Swim: Tips and Tricks for Machinists, Welders and Fabricators*. New York, NY: Industrial Press, 2009.

Learn all about metalworking from an expert in the field. Lipton's book offers handy tips, tricks, and techniques with stories and illustrations.

Nee, John G. *Fundamentals of Tool Design.* 6th ed. Dearborn, MI: Society of Manufacturing Engineers, 2010.
If tool design is of interest, this book is key to learning how to be a success in the business. Lots of illustrations, design examples, and a guide to machine tools are just a few of the highlights of this book.

PERIODICALS

American Tool, Die & Stamping News
42400 Grand River, Suite 103
Novi, MI 48375-2572
(800) 783-3491
Web site: http://www.ameritooldie.com
This magazine serves tool and die makers by presenting articles directly related to the craft. Each issue features news and current information for those wanting to know more about tool and die making.

Metalworking Insiders' Report
P.O. Box 107
Larchmont, NY 10538
(914) 834-2300
Web site: http://www.metalworkinginsider.info
For an all-encompassing periodical about the business of metalworking, this is a good bet. This magazine features articles about factory equipment—machine tools, controls, tooling, automation, and software—from all over the world.

Tooling and Production
P.O. Box 866
Osprey, FL 34229-0866
(941) 966-9521
E-mail: tooling@aip.com
Web site: http://www.toolingandproduction.com
This monthly magazine specializes in the metalworking
   industry. It provides information on products, indus-
   try trends, and techniques.

BLOGS
Tool and Dye
toolnddye.blogspot.com
Plenty of diagrams and illustrations accompany detailed
   articles about working with tools and dies. Some of
   the information is geared toward those already familiar with the work, but these posts give any reader an
   insight into the world of tool and die work.

MOVIES AND VIDEOS
Fundamentals of Machine Lathe Operation, 2004
Learn how to use one of the metalworking machines
   you might need for tool and die work under the instruction of a master machinist.

Troubleshooting Tool and Die Making, 2009
This short DVD guides viewers through a step-by-step process to help figure out what to do when things go wrong.

APPS

Sandvik Coromant Calculator

This app by Sandvik Coromant for machines and tooling helps users get accurate readings and measurements for cuts with turning, milling, and drilling applications.

TinkerBox

Try out some physics with this fun game app by Autodesk. Build machines, create inventions, and learn about mechanical concepts with puzzles.

CHAPTER 2

WORKING AS AN AUTO MECHANIC

Many people repair their own cars or want to learn how a car runs. Some turn this hobby into a living fixing cars. Automobiles are almost everywhere, so mechanics are in high demand, too. In addition, the U.S. Department of Labor reports that future opportunities are expected to be good for skilled mechanics.

WHAT AN AUTO MECHANIC DOES

Many car owners need a good auto mechanic to install new brakes or mount and repair tires. Automotive service technicians and mechanics inspect, maintain, and repair cars and trucks that are brought in for work. To fix a car that is not running properly, a mechanic has to figure out what's going wrong. He or she asks the car's owner for details about the car's problems, as well as what they were doing or what was happening when the problem occurred. Using this information, the mechanic goes through the proper steps, usually using special tools, computers, and diagnostic equipment, to diagnose what needs fixing.

Some mechanics perform routine service, which involves checking the whole vehicle to make sure everything is working properly, like brakes and hoses, and looking for potential problems.

Cars and trucks need certain work to make sure they keep running well. This is called routine service, and it works much differently than repairs. Most mechanics have a checklist of basic things to look for when servicing vehicles. They follow the list, examining the car and its parts, ensuring that the car is in proper working order, and fixing the things that aren't, such as plugs, hoses, and brake and fuel systems. Inspections can catch small problems before they become major issues or cause an accident.

OTHER MECHANIC JOBS

Another option for car and truck lovers is to work as an auto body repairer or repair service estimator. Automotive body repair involves fixing dents or problems on the outside of a car. Repairers make the car's exterior look like new after an accident with a new bumper or door panel. Sometimes they do fancy work like pin striping or flame designs.

Some mechanics work in professional racing as part of the pit crew. People in the pit have to be fast and accurate so that the race car driver can speed back on the track as fast as possible. Other mechanics specialize in special engines called diesel engines. Diesel engines power buses, trucks, and heavy equipment like cranes and bulldozers. Some passenger cars run on diesel, too. A diesel mechanic may work on the electrical system in the vehicle, the engine, or even adapt the engine so that it creates less pollution.

A repair service estimator checks an automobile and determines what needs to be fixed and estimates the cost of repair. Some workers specialize in automobile glass. They repair, refinish, or replace glass in cars and trucks. They are often called in after an accident to replace or repair broken windows or windshields. Automotive body repairers fix and replace bodies and bumpers on all kinds of vehicles.

Small engine mechanics work on all kinds of power equipment, such as motorcycles, boats, and other outdoor power equipment. Large or heavy vehicles need repairs, too. Heavy vehicle and mobile equipment service technicians work on vehicles and machinery used in industries such as construction, farming, and rail transportation. Some people like to restore and maintain old classic cars, too.

Automotive technology is constantly getting more sophisticated. Computers run our cars more every year (in fact, the first spaceship had fewer computers than a car does today!). Computers help make our automobiles run more efficiently and safely, and they make driving and riding in them more enjoyable. Automotive mechanics must understand electronic and computer systems, too. More cars run on alternative fuels, such as ethanol and electricity. Learning and using these new systems is challenging. Mechanics who have the skills to repair these complex systems are often called service technicians. There are so many parts to today's cars that some mechanics specialize in working on certain parts of them.

Automobiles today are more complex than ever, with computers running much of the engine functions. Therefore, a good training program is necessary for anyone wanting to go into the field.

TRAINING

Revving up a career in the automotive repair industry demands good math, electronics, and computer skills. More complex car systems require the mechanic to study up on and work with new, intricate technologies. For this reason, a training program of some kind is almost always necessary. Some high schools offer classes in automotive repair, electronics, computers, and mathematics, but not all schools teach the newest technologies. Most community colleges and technical school programs combine classroom training with actual repair work, which provides a thorough understanding of the inner workings of an automobile and how to fix even the most technologically complex cars and trucks. Programs can last anywhere from six months to two years. Some learn by helping or working with experienced mechanics. Training programs help auto mechanics quickly and accurately diagnose car problems. The more they know, the more efficiently they can fix the car. People want to leave the shop with their car running smoothly.

THE GOOD, THE BAD, AND THE UGLY

People who enjoy tinkering with cars and figuring out what makes them tick could work as auto mechanics and get paid for doing what they love. Also, because many employers want their workers to learn the newest methods for auto repair, they send them to classes.

Some repair shops can be dirty, with lots of greasy parts and tools. Lighting may not be very good, and the shop can be cold in the wintertime. With tools and parts lying around, it can be easy to slip and fall. Machines can be very loud, too. With that said, plenty of automotive repair shops are kept clean and are safe, so mechanics should choose a work-place where they'll feel comfort-able spending their days.

Mechanics need to lift heavy parts, and sometimes they have to remain in uncomfortable posi-tions for long periods of time. For example, they may have to work under a car, stretching up to reach a certain part. Auto mechanics should be strong and have a lot of energy to put into their work.

Auto mechanics may want to learn about the computers and electronics that make vehicles run. Some high schools teach the basics, and students can learn more at technical schools.

FOR MORE INFORMATION

ORGANIZATIONS

Automotive Service Association, Inc. (ASA)
8190 Precinct Line Road, Suite 100
Colleyville, TX 76034-7675
(800) 272-7467
Web site: http://www.asashop.org
The Automotive Service Association is a fifty-year-old organization with more than twelve thousand members. It promotes education and knowledge of car mechanics by making resources available to its members.

Automotive Youth Education Systems (AYES)
101 Blue Seal Drive, SE
Suite 101
Leesburg, VA 20175
(703) 669-6677
Web site: https://www.ayes.org
AYES is a nonprofit organization that seeks to help students get ready for automotive careers by exploring career options and developing and practicing the technical, academic, and employment skills they'll need.

Women's Automotive Association International
P.O. Box 2535
Birmingham, MI 48012
(248) 646-5250
Web site: http://www.waai.com
This organization focuses on women and their role in the automotive industry. It supports women in the

automotive industry by offering support, information, and scholarships to women with an interest in an automotive-related career.

WEB SITES

Due to the changing nature of Internet links, Rosen Publishing has developed an online list of Web sites related to the subject of this book. This site is updated regularly. Please use this link to access the list:

http://www.rosenlinks.com/CCWC/Build

BOOKS

Ginger, Helen. *TechCareers: Automotive Technicians.*
    Waco, TX: TSTC Publishing, 2009.
If the technology of cars interests you, check out this
    book to see if a career in this field is a good choice.

Orr, Tamra B. *A Career as an Auto Mechanic.* New York,
    NY: Rosen Publishing Group, 2010.
Learn all kinds of information on the career options for
    an auto mechanic, including the surprisingly wide
    range of vehicles you could work on.

Sclar, Deanna. *Auto Repair for Dummies.* 2nd ed. India-
    napolis, IN: For Dummies, 2008.
Anyone interested in learning what makes an engine rev
    can read all about the systems that make the car run,
    with information about repairs at the end of each section.

PERIODICALS

Car and Driver
1585 Eisenhower Place
Ann Arbor, MI 48108
(734) 971-3600
E-mail: editors@caranddriver.com
Web site: http://www.caranddriver.com
Car and Driver presents reviews of automobiles, articles
about automobiles, and industry news.

Motor Trend
P.O. Box 420235
Palm Coast, FL 32142-0235
(800) 274-1971
Web site: http://www.motortrend.com
Motor Trend has all the latest news on award-winning
cars, the newest cars, classic cars, and auto shows.

Underhood Service
3550 Embassy Parkway
Akron, OH 44333
(330) 670-1234
Web site: http://www.underhoodservice.com
In *Underhood Service,* you can read all about auto products, technical articles, and training information, as
well as watch helpful tech videos.

APPS

Car Paint Repair
This app by DroidReloaded guides users through the process of repairing scratches and chips to their vehicle's

paint. Learn about sanding methods, safety techniques, and how to repair scuffs, just to name a few.

The Mechanic. 1.0
Learn how to fix common vehicle problems with this free app by Charbel Toumieh. With information for all levels of expertise, users will find plenty to learn.

BLOGS

PopMech Proving Ground
www.popularmechanics.com/cars/news/auto-blog
If it's about automobiles, readers will likely find it on this blog. Check out *Popular Mechanics'* blog for news on the latest cars, car repair, and the newest cars out on the road.

MOVIES AND VIDEOS

Tell Me How Career Series: Auto Mechanic, 2012
Explore career opportunities, watch features about real people doing real jobs, and learn about training and challenges faced by auto mechanics, including the use of computers in today's automobiles.

TIG Welding Basics, 2007
Tungsten inert gas (TIG) welding is a versatile way to fuse metals together, which might come in handy when working on cars. Learn about the basics from master welder Ron Covell.

Workshop Safety: Auto Shop, 2008
This video for high school students shows what a garage is like and how to work safely in an auto shop.

CHAPTER 3

WORKING AS A CONSTRUCTION WORKER

According to the U.S. Department of Labor, the construction industry should continue to grow faster than any other occupation. Every day, more schools, office buildings, factories, and power plants go up, and others need maintenance. Construction workers build and maintain every home and business we enter and even the roads and bridges we travel. People will always need new structures, and these structures will need to be repaired and restored. Construction workers tend to be very well paid for all their hard work, too.

WHAT CONSTRUCTION WORKERS DO

Construction is generally made up of three parts. General building contractors build basic residential structures, such as houses, schools, stores, and office buildings. Heavy construction contractors work on major nonresidential projects, such as highways, bridges, and railroads. Plumbers, electricians, and carpenters are all special trade contractors. They focus on one area of construction, not the entire building.

Contractors supervise the building of a structure and hire subcontractors, or people who perform different tasks. They usually have plenty of skills and experience from their years in the business to manage the overall construction process, especially the details, such as how much it costs to rent special machinery. Contractors need to know what duties need to be performed before a structure can be complete and what order they need to be completed in, as well as how to hire the appropriate people to do different jobs and keep the job within budget.

Contractors should know the whole construction process because they supervise entire projects, including what jobs need to be done, whom to hire, and costs associated with the work.

TRAINING

Construction workers often start out as apprentices, studying and learning the job under a skilled worker. In return, they are expected to help out with small tasks, like carrying supplies. Helpers to skilled construction workers perform some of the heavy lifting and cleaning up. It's hard work but a great way to learn the job if you like the work.

Many companies send new workers to join and train with a union, where they spend several months on the job and in the classroom. When they return, they work as an

One way to get started in construction is to work with an experienced construction worker. In exchange, new workers may be asked to do some basic tasks.

apprentice. Apprenticeship programs are also available through specialty schools and colleges. No matter which route you choose, you'll start slowly, learning how to use simple machinery.

THE GOOD, THE BAD, AND THE UGLY

Construction is a great field to work in because the construction industry exists everywhere in the world. Besides job security, workers are also well paid for their hard work. Some construction workers are self-employed, so they also may have the best boss: themselves. Self-employed workers have the freedom to decide when they'll work and which jobs to accept.

Frank Thierbecker III has been working construction since he graduated from high school. One of the best parts of being a construction worker, he says, is that his job duties vary every day, depending on the area of construction he is working in or the job at hand.

The downsides to being a construction worker are often physical. "It's a lot of hard work," says Thierbecker, "and it's messy." Building big structures requires carrying large, and sometimes heavy, equipment and materials. It's important to be in good physical shape because workers do a lot of heavy lifting and carrying, sometimes for long periods of time.

OTHER CONSTRUCTION CAREERS

Another job option within construction is heavy equipment operator. Someone has to know how to operate huge backhoes, cranes, or pile drivers often seen on construction sites. These machines are used to move materials, earth, and other heavy things. Heavy equipment operators often need to get a license. Like other careers, beginners learn by working with a more experienced operator, often through an apprenticeship. More complicated machines require more training time. Workers pass a test for a license, and they're on their way.

Not sure about cruising around a construction site in a loud, hulking backhoe? There are plenty of job options to explore in the construction industry:

- Boilermakers
- Brickmasons, blockmasons, and stonemasons
- Carpenters
- Carpet installers
- Cement masons and terrazzo workers
- Construction and building inspectors
- Construction equipment operators
- Construction laborers and helpers
- Drywall and ceiling tile installers and tapers
- Electricians
- Elevator installers and repairers
- Glaziers
- Hazardous materials (hazmat) removal workers
- Insulation workers

- Oil and gas workers
- Painters
- Plasterers and stucco masons
- Plumbers, pipefitters, and steamfitters
- Reinforcing iron and rebar workers
- Roofers
- Sheet metal workers
- Structural iron and steel workers
- Tile and marble setters

The Bureau of Labor Statistics' *Occupational Outlook Handbook* has more information on all of these job options.

If the idea of being stuck indoors sounds dreadful, many construction jobs require a lot of time outside, especially if the job involves the construction of a road or bridge. That's great in sunny, warm weather. But the job is far less pleasant when the thermometer plummets below freezing, the wind is howling, or even if the sun is scorching. No matter what the weather, construction workers have to get the job done.

Working in the construction industry can be dangerous. Many tools used to build things can be harmful if used incorrectly or if there is an accident. Injured construction workers might not be able to do the work anymore and have to find a new job. Proper training can help prevent serious injuries.

Construction work is for all kinds of people, too. According to the National Association of Women in Construction (NAWIC), women make up about 9 percent of workers in the

Although men have filled most jobs in the industry, plenty of women lead successful construction careers, from laborers to managers.

construction industry. Within this field, 828,000 workers are women. The NAWIC was founded in 1953 by a group of sixteen female construction workers. Over the years, their membership has expanded to include thousands of women, and they have chapters all over the United States, parts of Canada, and beyond. So if you think that construction work is reserved for men, think again.

FOR MORE INFORMATION

ORGANIZATIONS

Associated Builders and Contractors (ABC)
4250 N. Fairfax Drive, 9th Floor
Arlington, VA 22203-1607
(703) 812-2000
Web site: http://www.abc.org
Associated Builders and Contractors is a national trade
   organization that strives to ensure top-of-the-line
   craftsmanship. The association has chapters across
   the country and offers safety programs to members
   of the organization.

National Association of Home Builders (NAHB)
1201 15th Street NW
Washington, DC 20005
(800) 368-5242
Web site: http://www.nahb.com
This organization's main goal is to ensure that safe
   buildings are built and that there is affordable hous-
   ing available to everyone.

WEB SITES

Due to the changing nature of Internet links, Rosen Publishing has developed an online list of Web sites related
to the subject of this book. This site is updated regularly.
Please use this link to access the list:

http://www.rosenlinks.com/CCWC/Build

BOOKS

Ching, Francis D. K. *Building Construction Illustrated*. 4th
ed. Hoboken, NJ: John Wiley & Sons, 2014.
This is a classic construction book to introduce readers
to the basic rules of building construction. Full of illustrations and drawings, readers will learn about different materials, building codes, and sustainability.

La Bella, Laura. *Internship & Volunteer Opportunities for
People Who Love to Build Things*. New York, NY: Rosen
Classroom, 2012.
One of the best ways to find out if a career in construction
is for you is to try it out. This book is a great overview of
many different volunteer opportunities and internships
out there, as well as how to get these positions.

Senker, Cath. *Construction Careers*. Mankato, MN:
Amicus, 2011.
Read all about what it's like to work in construction
with personal diaries from construction workers and
honest accounts of the good and the bad about
working this job.

PERIODICALS

Building Design + Construction
Circulation Department

3030 W. Salt Creek Lane, Suite 201
Arlington Heights, IL 60005-5025
(847) 391-1000
Web site: http://www.bdcnetwork.com
Building Design + Construction magazine seeks to provide important solutions that inspire construction
workers of every kind to design and build great places. Its site includes information on continuing education, blogs, videos, and more.

McGraw-Hill Construction
McGraw-Hill International Customer Service
860 Taylor Station Road
Blacklick, OH 43004
(609) 426-5793
Web site: http://www.construction.com
This magazine is for just about anyone in the construction industry. It provides readers with construction
projects and product information, plans and specifications, industry news, market research, and industry
developments.

APPS
Builders Construction Calculators, Estimators, and Planners
Create complete plans for all kinds of projects with this
app by Blocklayer.com, as well as calculate measurements and make conversions.

BLOGS

Hard Hat News

http://www.hardhat.com

This blog is for workers in heavy construction: excavating contractors, construction demolition, underground utility construction, landscaping, paving, and bridge construction.

MOVIES AND VIDEOS

American Experience: Building the Alaska Highway, 2005

Learn about one of the most ambitious projects ever undertaken: building the Alaskan highway.

Backhoe Basics, 2009

This brief video takes viewers through the basics of operating a backhoe. A great source for getting a sense of what it might be like to be a heavy machinery operator.

CHAPTER 4

WORKING AS A CARPENTER

If an afternoon dreaming up crazy creations and making them out of Lincoln Logs, Legos, or other building sets sounds like fun, consider a career in carpentry. Carpenters usually build or repair structures made of wood for commercial or residential buildings. They might work on the frame for a house or building, stairways, or kitchen cupboards. Some carpenters even work on highways and bridges.

WHAT CARPENTERS DO

Carpenters are just one type of construction worker, and many of their tasks have to do with building construction. With such variety in the trade, carpenters are almost always doing something different from one day to the next. Carpenters may be hired to construct door frames, hardwood floors, kitchen cabinets, and even insulate office buildings. Sometimes they work inside a home, installing drywall. Other times, they install exterior trim outside.

Carpentry offers a wide variety of job opportunities for workers in this industry. They might build frames for buildings, work inside on different parts of the structure, or even build furniture.

Some carpenters build furniture, such as tables and chairs. Other times they're hired to replace floor tiles or windowpanes. These carpenters have much more job flexibility because their work involves almost anything, not just buildings.

Such a vast array of jobs means carpenters use all kinds of tools and materials. Many hand tools, like levels and hammers, are useful in this trade. Some jobs require power tools such as drills and nail guns. Most carpenters keep a measuring tape within reach so that they can easily check a measurement.

Carpenters' jobs vary widely, but many carpenters consult blueprints and building plans for the specifics about what they are building. Using the details in the blueprints or plans, carpenters cut and measure wood or other materials using materials such as nails, glue, and screws. Carpenters always check

AN INTERVIEW WITH CARPENTER JONATHAN CLEMENT

Jonathan Clement, who presently works for Western Building Restoration in Albany, New York, has worked on "all aspects of carpentry, from building houses, to putting additions on, to remodeling houses…gutting them out, and doing the whole thing. And everything in between."

Clement started out cleaning up messes and carrying lumber. He learned gradually, but by the end of the summer, he was learning to build house frames. "Truthfully, I started this when I was about ten years old. My father was a carpenter, so to help me out and keep me out of trouble, he took me to work. I think the first day working with him I said, 'This is what I want to do for the rest of my life. I don't want to go to school anymore.' That's how I felt, and I never changed my mind. People said, 'When you get out of school, you're going to wish that you were back. You're going to wish that you spent more time, took it more seriously.' I said, 'I doubt it.' And I never did.

"When I first started with [my dad], he was building new houses, so he brought me to work …I was sweeping up behind him, carrying lumber. You know, probably at the end of that summer I was helping him frame. I was nailing walls together and climbing up on the roof.…I just took to it."

Clement's father gave him "on-the-job training, as it came up. He started out slow…I was really interested, and said, 'I want to do more than this.' When I wasn't working with my father, I was at home and building stuff around the house, building forts."

their work to make sure all cuts and measurements are correct and that everything has been put together the right way.

For any of this work, they must read plans and specifications for the buildings they work on. These are similar to blueprints, which can be challenging to read without proper training. Carpenters should be familiar with a structure's airflow management and insulation methods.

TRAINING

A carpenter is encouraged to get started in the field by completing an apprenticeship, where he or she will work with a skilled carpenter on the job, while simultaneously spending time in the classroom to learn about lessons in safety, first aid, different carpentry practices and skills, blueprint reading, mathematics, and drawing. This combination means workers are well trained and learn the practical skills they need to be successful woodworkers. Plenty of information on apprenticeship programs is available through the United Brotherhood of Carpenters and Joiners of America. Certain schools offer certification programs, too, but graduates still start out as apprentices on the job. In most states trained apprentices must pass a licensing test to get permits for jobs. The test is made up of questions testing applicants' knowledge of carpentry, including safety.

One of the best ways to start building experience in carpentry is to work with or observe someone who has been in the business for a while.

Most carpenters learn the trade on the job. Working under a skilled carpenter teaches new carpenters all about woodworking. By observing and helping a carpenter with many years of experience, workers can learn important skills that are necessary to be a success in the trade. Local hobby shops might have some recommendations for a school or center offering woodworking classes. Or simply look in the local phone book to find community colleges or recreation centers that have classes on woodworking or carpentry.

THE GOOD, THE BAD, AND THE UGLY

One of the most satisfying parts of working as a carpenter is being able to stand back and see the creation at the end of a project. Carpenters build things that will be a part of peoples' lives and homes for many years, which can make the work extra satisfying.

It may be interesting and varied, but carpentry requires a lot of hard, physical work. It involves bending, stretching, lifting, and kneeling. Carpenters may spend hours on their feet. Materials and tools may be heavy and awkward to carry. Some carpentry work is indoors, like in kitchens or living rooms, but plenty of carpentry requires days or weeks outside in the rain, snow, wind, or hot sun.

The most important rule in carpentry is "safety first." Carpenters work with tools that can cause serious injuries if they are not handled and used properly. Carpenters always have to focus on their work. The risk of danger is lessened by the knowledge of the tools of the trade and following proper safety precautions. They must also be careful on ladders to avoid falling and lift heavy materials with care.

FOR MORE INFORMATION

ORGANIZATIONS

Associated General Contractors of America (AGC)
2300 Wilson Boulevard, Suite 400
Arlington, VA 22201
(703) 548-3118
Web site: http://www.agc.org
This organization strives to support construction professionals and provide information on upcoming industry events. A magazine, newsletter, videos, and books relating to the construction trades are among some of its offerings.

Home Builders Institute (HBI)
1201 15th Street NW, 6th Floor
Washington, DC 20005
(202) 371-0600
Web site: http://www.hbi.org
The Home Builders Institute provides education and training, as well as apprenticeship programs for those wanting to learn more about the construction trades. It works with the National Association of Home Builders to develop the construction trade.

United Brotherhood of Carpenters and Joiners of America
101 Constitution Avenue NW
Washington, DC 20001
Web site: https://www.carpenters.org
The United Brotherhood of Carpenters and Joiners of

America is one of the oldest labor unions. Today, it is one of the biggest building trade unions in North America.

WEB SITES

Due to the changing nature of Internet links, Rosen Publishing has developed an online list of Web sites related to the subject of this book. This site is updated regularly. Please use this link to access the list:

http://www.rosenlinks.com/CCWC/Build

BOOKS

Corbett, Stephen. *The Complete Illustrated Guide to Woodworking*. London, England: Southwater Publishing, 2013.
Try out one or all of more than thirty basic woodworking projects to start learning new skills in carpentry.

Miller, Jeff. *The Foundations of Better Woodworking: How to Use Your Body, Tools and Materials to Do Your Best Work*. New York, NY: Popular Woodworking Books, 2012.
This book covers the essentials, such as getting to know your materials, how to stand to make better cuts, and explanations about how to cut a line.

Roza, Greg. *A Career as a Carpenter*. New York, NY: Rosen Publishing Group, 2010.
This book gives an overview of the career, tips on finding apprenticeships, educational opportunities, and much more.

PERIODICALS

Fine Woodworking
The Taunton Press, Inc.
63 South Main Street
P.O. Box 5506
Newtown, CT 06470-5506
(203) 426-8171
Web site: http://www.finewoodworking.com
Fine Woodworking specializes in providing information to carpenters, craftsmen, and furniture makers. It includes informative articles to help you learn more about working with wood.

Popular Woodworking Magazine
P.O. Box 421751
Palm Coast, FL 32142-1751
(855) 840-5118
Web site: http://www.popularwoodworking.com
Check out articles and tips from woodworking pros on projects for beginners to professionals. Watch old shows and read back issues of the magazine on its Web site.

APPS

Fine Woodworking
Experience *Fine Woodworking*, America's premier woodworking resource, on an iPad and enjoy the full magazine, plus bonus features and digital enhancements embedded in every digital issue: linkable and

searchable content, technique videos, slide shows, tutorials, inspiring photo galleries, and more.

BLOGS

Building Moxie

http://www.buildingmoxie.com

This blog has tips and other information for any carpenter, whether he or she is at home or on the job. It includes plenty of home maintenance hints, new styles and technologies, and how-to discussions to keep readers interested and informed.

Full Chisel

http://www.fullchisel.com/blog

Anyone interested in carpentry using hand tools will find plenty of photos, diagrams, and frank discussions about using hand tools this blog was listed as one of the top one hundred carpentry blogs.

MOVIES AND VIDEOS

Measure Twice, Cut Once: Essential Building Basics for Kids of All Ages, 2008

This DVD teaches viewers building basics and how to build a tree fort at the same time.

Hand Tools: Tuning and Using Chisels, Planes and Saws, 2006

From the publishers of *Fine Woodworking* magazine, this DVD teaches new carpenters how to use some of the basic tools of the trade.

CHAPTER 5

WORKING AS A PLUMBER

Plumbers are a necessary service everywhere. People depend on water, and when it doesn't run in their homes, they call a reliable plumber. Every modern commercial and residential building has a plumbing system. And with new buildings being constructed all the time, work is always available for an experienced and skilled plumber.

Plumbers keep the water supply safe and clean. An often-heard motto, "Plumbers protect the health of the nation," says it all. To make good on that motto, they put in a whole lot of time, energy, and hard work. Plumbers are respected and essential everywhere.

WHAT PLUMBERS DO

For plumbers, every day is different. Some days they install sinks in new homes. Other days they are called to fit pipes into a bathroom or kitchen. And sometimes they even get the chance to install new hot water and steam boilers, which are required to maintain heat in a house. They might be called at 3 AM for an emergency, such as burst or frozen pipes, or work overtime to finish a job.

Most of a plumber's work deals with the pipes that move water and waste into and out of houses and buildings. Some plumbing systems are behind walls, so plumbers may cut into walls to access the pipes and repair or perform maintenance. They also have to cut pipes and join them back together using clamps, screws, bolts, cement, or solder. Every plumber should have excellent organizational skills. Plumbing systems need to be orderly so that anyone who works on the system can easily understand how it was put together. Of course, maintenance is also a big part of the plumber's job.

Any time a new house or other structure is built, plumbers are needed to install the plumbing fixtures and systems. A plumber installs the sink as well as appliances like dishwashers and garbage disposals in a new kitchen. Wherever there is a need for water to be carried throughout a building, a plumber is the person to call for help.

TRAINING

Many plumbers learn about the trade through an apprenticeship, and some get their start by attending a technical school. For thirty-four years, Richard Noble has been a plumber in New Jersey. To become a plumber, he says, "It takes five years

Plumbers often use a torch to heat and melt solder that joins copper pipes together. Pipes can also be made of steel or plastic.

of practical experience in the plumbing trade, working under a journeyman (experienced) plumber. After five years, you apply for a state license and then take a test. The test is all about the plumbing code, which specifies what is required by law for the installation of water lines, waste and vent lines, and building structures."

Most plumbers learn all about the trade by working as a plumber's helper. Helpers are sometimes stuck with hard,

POP STAR PLUMBERS

The inventor of the toilet was John Harrington. Back in 1596, Harrington created the flushing toilet. He was actually employed as a writer and wrote an amusing article called "Plan Plots of a Privy of Perfection." He planned out and put together a flushing water closet for his godmother, Queen Elizabeth I. She was thrilled! It would be a few hundred years before it became popular, but the creative ideas started flowing.

Albert Einstein once announced that he would have been a plumber if he hadn't become a physicist. The Plumbers and Steamfitters Union made him an honorary member. Rock and roller Ozzy Osborne was once a plumber, too. Actors such as Sir Michael Caine, who starred in *The Dark Knight*, among many other films, started out in a career as a plumber before he made the leap to acting. Also Bob Hoskins, who was in the movies *Hook* and *Who Framed Roger Rabbit?*, made a living as a plumber before he became a famous actor. In fact, he has even played plumbers in some of his films.

dirty work, such as carrying some of the plumber's heavy equipment and other smaller plumbing duties, but they get great hands-on experience. Once a helper learns the many different tasks a plumber must be able to do, he or she can go on to be a full-fledged plumber.

THE GOOD, THE BAD, AND THE UGLY

Many plumbers feel good about helping people with this important service. Also, for people who enjoy building things, getting a kitchen or bathroom in working order is a method of building something. Plumbers create something that operates

Plumbing can be exhausting work under tough conditions. Building the plumbing for a kitchen, however, can make plumbing a very satisfying job.

by planning ahead and using the proper tools and their knowledge of plumbing.

Of course, not every day is smooth and easy. Some days are long and exhausting. Some days, a plumber has to carry a 350-pound (159-kilogram) bathtub up a flight of stairs. Plumbers have to be strong and ready to spend a lot of time on their feet. There isn't much time to rest or sit down. They have to carry their equipment with them, and many plumbing supplies, such as water heaters and metal pipes, are heavy. Plumbers have to climb ladders, too. They sometimes have to work outdoors, even if the weather is bad.

People who enjoy seeing physical proof of a completed task might appreciate this career. Plumbers get to see their work in action after their labor is done. Noble says, "The best part is being able to see the end product of your labor, in the form of a new bathroom or kitchen."

FOR MORE INFORMATION

ORGANIZATIONS

International Association of Plumbing and
Mechanical Officials (IAPMO)
4755 E. Philadelphia Street
Ontario, CA 91761
(909) 472-4100
E-mail: iapmo@iapmo.org
Web site: http://www.iapmo.org
The IAPMO sets codes to deliver the most secure and
effective methods of installing plumbing.

Plumbing-Heating-Cooling Contractors Association
180 S. Washington Street
Falls Church, VA 22046
(703) 237-8100
Web site: http://www.phccweb.org
The Plumbing-Heating-Cooling Contractors Association
strives to advance and educate the plumbing and
HVACR industry for society's health, safety, and com-
fort as well as protecting the environment.

WEB SITES

Due to the changing nature of Internet links, Rosen Publishing has developed an online list of Web sites related

to the subject of this book. This site is updated regularly. Please use this link to access the list:

http://www.rosenlinks.com/CCWC/Build

BOOKS

Cauldwell, Rex. *Plumbing Complete: Expert Advice from Start to Finish*. Newtown, CT: The Taunton Press, 2009.
Plenty of photographs and clear, detailed steps walk any plumber through home repairs and installations, whether they're simple or more complicated. Tips on what to do when something goes wrong help the reader along.

Creative Homeowner Editors. *Ultimate Guide: Plumbing*. 3rd ed. Upper Saddle River, NJ: Creative Homeowner, 2010.
Newly updated and expanded, *Ultimate Guide: Plumbing* reviews the latest plumbing products and techniques together with overviews of code-compliant plumbing methods.

Creative Publishing Editors. *The Complete Guide to Plumbing*. 5th ed. Minneapolis, MN: Creative Publishing International, 2012.

This book provides all the information you need to complete basic plumbing installations and repairs, more complicated renovations, and even winterization methods.

PERIODICALS

Bath & Kitchen Pro
BNP Media
2401 W. Big Beaver Road, Suite 700
Troy, MI 48084
(248) 362-3700
Web site: http://www.bathandkitchenpro.com
Bath & Kitchen Pro is for professionals who buy, install, and replace bath-and-kitchen products and systems. It also covers industry news, product information, and a blog.

Plumbing and Mechanical
2401 W. Big Beaver Road, Suite 700
Troy, MI 48084
(248) 362-3700
Web site: http://www.pmmag.com
This magazine provides information on plumbing, including product reviews, plumbing news, and current plumbing concerns.

APPS

Plumbing Professional

The Plumbing Professional app by Multieducator, Inc., puts international plumbing codes, more than eighty formulas, and conversions at its users' fingertips for handy reference on-the-go.

BLOGS

Master Plumber

masterplumber.blogspot.com

Ronnie Jackson is a licensed plumber in California. On this blog, he offers his expertise to help everyone from beginning plumbers to experts looking to learn more. Posts include tips, links to useful sites, and stories.

MOVIES AND VIDEOS

Plumbing Projects 1-2-3, 2008

The Home Depot's video provides instructions on how to get started doing your own plumbing repairs around the house.

How to DYI: Plumbing, 2007

This video guides viewers through many plumbing projects and repairs around the house.

CHAPTER 6

WORKING AS AN ELECTRICIAN

Electricity is humming all the time, powering the alarm clocks that wake us up, the lights that brighten our homes, and the refrigerator that keeps our food fresh and cold. How different life would be without electricity. Electricians perform essential jobs; they install and repair electrical devices like heating, air-conditioning, lighting, and refrigeration. It's a complex and crucial job.

WHAT ELECTRICIANS DO

No structure is built without a plan for the electricity. Someone decides where it makes the most sense to install outlets, light fixtures, light switches, circuits, and other electrical elements. Blueprints show where to install electrical systems that light, heat, and cool the building, as well as cables for the computer and Internet.

Many kinds of wires connect these intricate electrical systems, which can quickly get complicated. Wires must be

Electricians have to be careful and organized all the time. They must know the right kinds of wire to use in each situation, as well as how to connect them.

carefully organized because when it comes time for repair or maintenance, the electrician needs to clearly recognize where everything is. Electricians must be organized at all times.

To properly install wires, electricians must know the right type of wire to use and the best way to connect it. Conduits are used in office buildings and other commercial buildings,

63

ELECTRIFYING!

Electricity can do some pretty amazing things, but death from electrocution is a real danger for electricians and construction workers. Many workers have been seriously injured or died while working near live wires. An electric shock can cause a slight irritation, but it can also lead to death. To avoid injury, electricians must always keep in mind how close they are working to live wires, whether they're power lines or wires in an attic crawlspace. Power lines are so full of electricity that even touching something else that is touching it can cause serious harm.

The potential for other injuries, such as burns, is high. Cuts and falls are real dangers as well. Safety goggles and protective clothing help electricians protect themselves. Electricians must follow strict safety guidelines to avoid serious injury or even death.

Modern wiring is well insulated, but before 1950 wires were only insulated by cloth. Some older homes and buildings still have their old wiring, which looks a lot like modern insulation, but cloth can break down and fall apart, causing fires from sparks or shocks to anyone who touches them.

Even the most conscientious electrician is at risk for hurting himself or herself. The majority of injuries happen at the end of a long day when workers are tired. They may occur when hurrying to finish up a job or when the blueprints are incorrect. Every electrician should be especially careful under these circumstances and avoid harm.

but plastic-covered wire is used in homes. The ends of the wires are connected by twisting the ends together using pliers or soldering them together with a soldering gun.

Electricians test all the wiring to guarantee that it was installed correctly and the electricity works properly. Ohm-meters, voltmeters, and oscilloscopes are all tools to test electricity.

Maintenance electricians repair and replace electrical systems in places that need a staff member to keep electricity working, such as hospitals, office buildings, college campuses, and factories. Of course, maintenance electricians make repairs when something malfunctions, but they also replace electrical systems and their parts before they break, such as updating wire in a home or repairing a hotel's electrical equipment. Generally, though, they inspect equipment and make sure the electrical systems run without problems.

TRAINING

Most people get their start as an electrician informally by working under an experienced electrician or by enrolling in an apprenticeship program. Electrician's helpers learn important safety practices and how to install and connect wires. The more they learn, the more responsibility they'll earn.

Electricians always learn about safety. Power lines conduct so much electricity that even touching something that is leaning against a wire can cause a major injury.

Apprenticeship training teaches new electricians all they need to know to practice the trade in four to five years. In the classroom students learn about electrical theory, blueprint reading, mathematics, and electrical code requirements. Apprentices may have an easier time finding a job; they are prepared to work in both construction and maintenance, and employers know they've had a thorough education.

Most states require electricians to have a license before they are considered a certified electrician. Getting a license usually means taking a test with questions ranging from safety precautions to electrical theory. Each state has its own requirements, so check with the state's licensing agency.

THE GOOD, THE BAD, AND THE UGLY

Work as an electrician or a maintenance electrician is available just about everywhere. Also, demand for skilled electricians to install, test, and repair electrical systems will continue as long as we rely on electricity.

Electricians often have to work in awkward or cramped surroundings to reach wires, sometimes standing for a long time. They work both indoors and outdoors.

Maintenance electricians generally have on-call hours, which means their schedule is open during certain hours in case something needs to be fixed right away. Electricians on construction sites may work overtime to meet deadlines.

FOR MORE INFORMATION

ORGANIZATIONS

National Electrical Contractors Association
3 Bethesda Metro Center, Suite 1100
Bethesda, MD 20814
(301) 657-3110
Web site: http://www.necanet.org
The National Electrical Contractors Association helps
those in the industry and those that want to learn
more about electrical construction. It publishes informative publications such as Electrical Contractor
magazine, has chapters around the world, and hosts a
career center for those looking for jobs or employees.

U.S. Department of Energy
1000 Independence Avenue SW
Washington, DC 20585
(202) 586-5000
E-mail: the.secretary@hq.doe.gov
Web site: http://www.energy.gov
The Department of Energy is a governmental organization that strives to provide and maintain a reliable energy system. It is concerned with environmental issues
and minimizing environmental waste.

WEB SITES

Due to the changing nature of Internet links, Rosen Publishing has developed an online list of Web sites related
to the subject of this book. This site is updated regularly.
Please use this link to access the list:

http://www.rosenlinks.com/CCWC/Build

BOOKS

Brickner, Dale E., and John E. Traister. *Electrician's Exam Preparation Guide*. Carlsbad, CA: Craftsman Book Company, 2008.
Anyone getting ready to take the electrician's exam will appreciate this source for sample test questions, actual past tests, and answer explanations.

Harmon, Daniel E. *A Career as an Electrician*. New York, NY: Rosen Classroom, 2010.
Readers learn about the duties and responsibilities, the variety of careers, helpful training, and how to begin and advance in an electrical career. This book includes interviews with professionals and sample exam questions from practice tests.

Shamieh, Cathleen, and Gordon McComb. *Electronics for Dummies*. 2nd ed. Hoboken, NJ: John Wiley and Sons, 2009.
This book is a great overall reference for students or those just learning about electronics. It explains the fundamentals of electronics.

PERIODICALS

Electrical Construction & Maintenance Magazine
9800 Metcalf Avenue
Overland Park, KS 66212
(913) 341-1300
E-mail: electrical.group@penton.com
Web site: http://www.ecmweb.com

Electrical Construction & Maintenance Magazine features information on electrical design, construction, operations, and the maintenance industry with in-depth technical articles, market/construction forecasts, proprietary surveys, late-breaking news stories, and comprehensive product reviews.

Electrical Line
Pacific Media Publishing, Inc.
1785 Emerson Court
North Vancouver, BC V7H 2Y6
Canada
(604) 924-3661
E-mail: sales@electricalline.com
Web site: http://www.electricalline.com
Electrical Line is a bimonthly publication for electricians operating in Canada. It includes industry news, product information, and articles about the industry.

APPS

Electrician Terminology 1.0
This app by William Patten helps students prepare for the electrician licensing exam. Anyone can use it to learn electrician terminology with a dictionary, quizzes, and flash cards.

Kidskool: Electrician 1.0
This app by Apps Capital Social Funding for all ages uses games to teach users about the tools and terms used by electricians.

BLOGS

EZ DIY Electricity
http://www.ezdiyelectricity.com
Wayne Gilchrist, a licensed master electrician in Montana, calls on more than twenty-two years of electrical trade experience to help readers safely and easily complete electrical wiring projects. It includes wiring diagrams, articles, e-books, and videos.

The Internet Electrician
internetelectrician.blogspot.com
Professional electrician Terry Peterman's blog is designed to share his knowledge and experience. Articles and videos provide information on performing home electrical repairs, renovations, or additions to existing electrical systems.

MOVIES AND VIDEOS

The Basics of Household Wiring, Electrical Video and Repair, 2008
This DVD features an illustrated training program to teach electrical wiring techniques, with procedures, practice techniques, and diagrams.

Convergence Training—Electrical Safety General Awareness, 2009
Safety is one of the most important tools for any electrician. This DVD covers personal protective equipment and electrical injuries such as shocks, burns, electrocutions, and falls.

CHAPTER 7

WORKING AS A GARDENER

Gardeners take care of lawns, flower gardens, vegetable beds, trees, and other flora. People who like planting and designing their own gardens or yard might enjoy becoming a gardener. Creating a garden or maintaining a piece of land results in a gorgeous creation that everyone will enjoy.

WHAT GARDENERS DO

Gardening careers are plentiful. Greenhouse workers work in a greenhouse, of course, where they plant and grow seeds for plants and trees until they're mature enough to be transplanted into the ground. Greenhouse workers learn about all kinds of plants, flowers, vegetables, and trees. They have a lot of freedom to try out new growing techniques.

Once the plants are mature enough, it's time for the landscape laborers to get those plants, trees, and shrubs into the ground to grow. They usually arrange plants and gardens based on a plan by a landscape designer and the owners. Landscape laborers move flowers from the nursery, plant them, care for

Plants and trees are sometimes started in a greenhouse, where greenhouse workers care for them until they have developed enough to be planted in a garden.

them, and make sure they stay healthy and attractive. "It helps to be able to identify basic plant groups when you're placing them," says landscaping foreman Ryan Niver. Landscape laborers also do a lot of garden and flowerbed preparation work, or "bed prep," by changing areas of lawn and woods into gardens. Landscape laborers also build hardscape, says Niver, which includes walls, walkways, patios, and sometimes driveways. Landscape laborers work at private homes and estates, and corporate buildings, as well as for cities and parks.

UNUSUAL GARDENS

Plants need sun, water, and soil to grow, right? Not so fast. Aquatic plants live completely underwater. Plants usually get the carbon dioxide they need from the air. Aquatic plants don't need air to live because they get the oxygen and food they need from the surrounding water and from photosynthesis. Water lilies and lotuses are a common example of floating plants used in pond gardens. Aquatic gardeners care for these plants. The Aquatic Gardeners Association can provide you with more information about these gardens.

Believe it or not, some gardens grow plants without using soil. The hydroponic method of gardening has been used for thousands of years: the hanging gardens of Babylon and the floating gardens of China are two early examples. Instead of soil, hydroponic gardening carries water and nutrients to the plant. These extra nutrients help the plant to flourish. They grow 30 to 50 percent faster, say the experts, probably because the roots get so much more oxygen. The lack of soil ensures fewer bugs and less disease, so hydroponically grown plants don't require as many pesticides as their soil-grown counterparts.

Vegetables, flowers, and herbs can all be grown without soil, but there are a number of ways to grow different kinds of plants this way. For example, deepwater culture grows small and medium-sized plants such as herbs and lettuce in a solution with lots of nutrients. Medium or large plants such as tomatoes and African violets may thrive in a nutrient film technique (NFT). With NFT, a thin layer, or film, of nutrients flow over the plants' roots.

Lawn service workers generally care for lawns. They may be responsible for cleaning up the lawn of a private residence, or commercial areas, such as banks or doctor's offices. They mow lawns, trim shrubbery, and make sure the lawn is healthy and green. The more experience with plants and flowers a person has, the better the gardener he or she can be.

TRAINING

It's easy to get a feel for some of the different gardening jobs: plant gardens or flower beds, mow the lawn, or trim the hedges. Working with supervisors provides on-the-job training to teach the skills for entry-level jobs, such as planting and taking care of gardens and lawns. Gardeners must listen, follow directions, and show enthusiasm.

Some employers may send employees to training programs to learn about landscape design, horticulture, arboriculture, and safety. In most states, people who work with pesticides must pass a test on their knowledge of safe use and proper disposal of pesticides.

Get into the dirt right away by learning all about plants and gardening. Plan out a garden in the yard, or plant herbs in a flowerpot on the kitchen windowsill or porch. Those who like lawn work can start their own lawn mowing services by working for friends and neighbors.

It's never too soon to start learning about the green world. Schools and organizations offer gardening classes for everyone. In New York City, for example, the Brooklyn Botanic Garden offers classes in their children's garden for kids ages two to seventeen. They work with garden instructors to plant and harvest their own crops. Older kids who complete the program can become junior instructors. The Berkshire Botanical garden offers "Farm in the Garden Camp" for five to ten year olds. Check the local phone book for schools in the area that offer these kinds of classes.

THE GOOD, THE BAD, AND THE UGLY

There are lots of gardening jobs available. Lawns always need mowing, vegetables and flowers need to be planted, and trees and shrubs need pruning all over the

In larger landscaping companies, the landscape construction crew is in charge of preparing the ground and soil for sod, rolls of grass that are sometimes used to start new lawns.

world. Work in this industry is seasonal, however, so jobs could be scarce in the northern areas during the winter months, when ice and snow prevent most plants from growing. Gardeners have to find another means of employment during these times, head to warmer climates, or make sure they've worked enough during nice weather to carry them through the winter.

Gardening is hard, dirty, challenging work. The work is usually outdoors most of the time, sometimes in very hot, rainy, or even cold weather. It requires a lot of physical strength and stamina. Gardeners bend down a lot, shovel, and carry heavy equipment. Inconveniences like these don't seem like such a big deal if you love your job, though.

FOR MORE INFORMATION

ORGANIZATIONS

National Gardening Association (NGA)
P.O. Box 4515
Burlington, VT 05406
(802) 863-5251
Web site: http://www.assoc.garden.org
The NGA works to renew and sustain the connection between people, plants, and the environment. The site features expert advice, a gardener's dictionary, and a weed library.

Professional Grounds Management Society
720 Light Street
Baltimore, MD 21230
(410) 223-2861
E-mail: pgms@assnhqtrs.com
Web site: http://www.pgms.org
This organization provides information on professional grounds management, with a focus on environmental awareness and keeping Earth healthy and safe.

Professional Landcare Network (PLANET)
950 Herndon Parkway, Suite 450
Herndon, VA 20170-5528
(800) 395-2522
Web site: http://www.landcarenetwork.org
PLANET is a national trade association for landscape industry professionals. Its site includes information about certification, safety, classes, and other education opportunities.

U.S. Department of Agriculture Cooperative State
Research, Education, and Extension Service1
400 Independence Avenue SW, Stop 2201
Washington, DC 20250-2201
(800) 333-4636
Web site: http://www.csrees.usda.gov/about/jobs.html
Check out this division of the USDA for plenty of information
about job options, including how to apply for federal jobs.

WEB SITES

Due to the changing nature of Internet links, Rosen Publishing has developed an online list of Web sites related to the subject of this book. This site is updated regularly. Please use this link to access the list:

http://www.rosenlinks.com/CCWC/Build

BOOKS

Ferguson Editors. *Landscaping and Horticulture*. New York, NY: Ferguson Publishing, 2008.
All kinds of jobs await those who would rather dig in the dirt and plant greens. This book outlines many options with job descriptions, career outlooks, and more.

Fox, Thomas. *Urban Farming: Sustainable City Living in Your Backyard, in Your Community, and in the World*. Irvine, CA: Bow Tie Press, 2011.
This book is a great source for anyone who wants to start gardening in the city.

Resh, Howard. *Hobby Hydroponics*. 2nd ed. Boca Raton, FL: CRC Press, 2013.

Think hydroponic gardening is just for professionals?
This book provides readers with tips and instructions
for beginners.

PERIODICALS

Fine Gardening
The Taunton Press, Inc.
63 South Main Street
P.O. Box 5506
Newtown, CT 06470
Web site: http://www.taunton.com/fg
If you love gardening, flip through the pages of *Fine
Gardening*. It includes tips on improving your garden,
videos, and information to help you improve your
gardening knowledge.

Organic Gardening
400 South Tenth Street
Emmaus, PA 18098-0099
(800) 666-2206
E-mail: ogdcustserv@rodale.com
Web site: http://www.organicgardening.com
This magazine Web site features all kinds of articles to
teach you about growing a natural, chemical-free garden: how to combat garden pests (and encourage the
beneficial ones!), building raised beds, and even keeping chickens! It offers free downloads, too.

APPS

Landscapers Companion
This app by Stevenson Software puts a reference guide

to trees, shrubs, and all sorts of plants right at the user's fingertips with information on more twenty-two thousand plants and fifteen-thousand pictures.

Leafsnap
Ever wonder what kind of tree that is in the park but are unable to look it up at home?
Researchers from Columbia University, the University of Maryland, and the Smithsonian Institution have created a free mobile app that helps identify tree species from photographs of their leaves.

BLOGS

A Way to Garden
http://www.awaytogarden.com
Former *Newsday* and *Martha Stewart Living* garden editor Margaret Roach invites readers into her garden with photos, plant information, recipes, and podcasts.

MOVIES AND VIDEOS

The Complete Gardener: Great Gardening Tips, 2007
This video offers helpful and unique tips for every gardener, whether you're working on several acres or a simple patio garden.

Five Secrets of Great Gardening, 2009
Learn all about horticultural design, water management and irrigation, pruning, pest management, and propagation in clearly explained techniques and tips.

CHAPTER 8

WORKING AS A SCULPTOR

All kinds of materials—clay, wire, glass, plastic, fabric, and ice, just to name a few—can be used by sculptors to build a piece of three-dimensional art. Sculptors love art as much as they like building things and find inspiration to create all around them. This job offers a lot of freedom.

Sculpting is a type of art that one can start learning right away. Some sculptures are simply made out of paper, so all one needs is paper and an idea. Although there is no specific way to build a sculpture, researching different techniques and tools may help start a career as a sculptor.

WHAT SCULPTORS DO

Sculpting is a type of fine art. Unlike other careers in art, such as graphic design or illustration, sculptors usually do not work for large corporations. Almost 70 percent of all sculptors are self-employed, so the work they do is generally for themselves. Sometimes this is called freelance work. Freelance sculptors do not have to work with anyone else's ideas

Sculptors can create their art out of almost anything, including metal, and those who work for themselves can use their imaginations to make what they want.

or plans. When sculptors work for themselves, they have the freedom to create art that is from their own imaginations.

Occasionally, sculptors may work on commission for an individual, a group, a corporation, or even a city, which pays them for their art. Commissioned works are not that common. So how do sculptors make a living creating art? They sometimes show their art in galleries where buyers can purchase their pieces. Artists might work with art dealers, who sell the artists' sculptures for them. Some sculptors work on their art part-time and hold another job as well, such as teaching or tutoring, especially as they are just getting started. Eventually, successful sculptors can open their own studios or galleries.

Sculptors use almost any kind of material to create their sculptures. Many stick to a single type of material, such as clay, glass, metal, or wood. Other sculptors use a variety of materials, such as sand, plastic, and even trash. Artists cut, glue, saw, solder, and mold materials into three-dimensional (3-D) sculptures.

TRAINING

Most public high schools offer art classes as an elective. By taking one of these art classes and working with the instructor, students can decide if they like it enough to keep at it. A job as a sculptor doesn't necessarily require going to college and getting formal training, however; one can certainly learn to sculpt by attending an art school.

As with any type of art, it may take years of practice to become a skilled sculptor. Beginning sculptors should explore all kinds of materials that can be used to sculpt and determine which ones they like to use. They should explore, experiment with, and practice the many sculpture techniques to better understand what kinds of sculpting can be done and the type they most enjoy. Some types of sculpture might require research, whether into the subject or the medium.

As a sculptor gets started in this business, he or she needs a lot of patience. It can take a long time to form a reputation and sell his or her work consistently enough to make a living from sculpting alone. Sculptors need plenty of enthusiasm and should resolve to work hard to get some recognition.

SCULPTURE FOR THE SCREEN

Sculpture is a small but important part of computer-animated movies. Sculptors are needed to create sculptures, or maquettes, of the characters. A special 3-D scanner records every tiny detail of the maquette into a computer. Some creatures are created right on the computer, but many start out as simple sculptures. Maquettes are scanned into a computer, and the scanned images are used to create computerized models. For example, in all of the *Lord of the Rings* movies, sculptors made large maquettes of some of the characters. Sometimes landscape scenes are made with a 3-D wire model.

Maquettes are also sculpted to make models for figurines and toys. Tony Cipriano is a freelance sculptor who makes toys and statues for both the animation industry and action figure companies. When he starts on a sculpture, Cipriano sometimes gets to come up with designs or a client may give him drawings. First he uses wire and a chunk of putty to make an armature, which is a frame he'll base his sculpture on. The wire is bent into the basic pose. Over this, he starts blocking in basic features, like the skull, rib cage, and pelvis, just using his hands. From here he'll begin using tools to start adding more and more detail, constantly stepping back from the sculpture and turning it.

For small sculptures, Cipriano makes a wax mold of his figure. The wax is much harder than clay, which makes it easier to add crisp detail, such as teeth and hair, to such small pieces. He uses a wax pen, which is heated, to add the final details to the wax sculpture.

Sculpture comes in all shapes and sizes. Alexander Calder's *Flamingo* is a bright, eye-catching sculpture in Chicago, Illinois. It stands 53 feet (16 meters) tall and weighs 50 tons!

Becoming a sculptor is more like a financially beneficial hobby or passion. Some sculptors sell their art to galleries or at craft fairs. Some open an online store on Web sites like Etsy, where people shop to buy unique, handmade crafts and art. The more persistent they are, the better their chances of selling their work.

THE GOOD, THE BAD, AND THE UGLY

Some artists say that the best thing about a career as a sculptor is that they love the work they do every day. It's easier to get out of bed in the morning when they're going to a job they enjoy.

A major draw to sculpting is that artists have no limitations to their work. They can be completely creative and make their sculpture as big or as small as they want. With mixed-media sculpture, they have even more options. Any material they can imagine can be worked into the piece. Some artists even use light and sound to create an experience that engages more than just sight—they captivate motion and sound or music.

Keep in mind, though, that it is hard to make a living without a steady paycheck. Long periods without selling a piece of art may make it hard to pay the bills. Though some artists may have to pick up a second job to pay bills, it is entirely possible to make a good living as a sculptor. They believe in their work and do their best to sell their art.

FOR MORE INFORMATION

ORGANIZATIONS

National Ice Carving Association (NICA)
P.O. Box 3593
Oak Brook, IL 60522-3593
(630) 871-8431
E-mail: nicaexdir@aol.com
The NICA promotes the art of ice sculpture or ice carving and provides education, business, and competitions around the world.

National Sculpture Society (NSS)
75 Varick Street, 11th Floor
New York, NY 10013
(212) 764-5645
Web site: http://www.nationalsculpture.org
The NSS promotes the knowledge of excellence in sculpture inspired by the natural world. Its members create, interpret, exhibit, collect and support the evolving tradition in American sculpture.

Sculptors Society of Canada (SSC)
500 Church Street
Toronto, ON M4Y 2C8
Canada
(647) 435-5858
E-mail: gallery@cansculpt.org
Web site: http://www.cansculpt.org
The SSC is dedicated to educating, promoting, and exhibiting young Canadian sculptors. It also seeks to educate the public about the fine art of sculpting.

WEB SITES

Due to the changing nature of Internet links, Rosen Publishing has developed an online list of Web sites related to the subject of this book. This site is updated regularly. Please use this link to access the list:

http://www.rosenlinks.com/CCWC/Build

BOOKS

Bruckner, Tim. *Pop Sculpture: How to Create Action Figures and Collectible Statues*. New York, NY: Watson-Guptill Publications, 2010.
This book covers every step in making sculptures for collectibles and figures. Readers will learn everything from research to sculpting to preparing the final product for sale.

Miles, Cathy. *Sculpting in Wire*. London, England: A&C Black, 2009.
Learn how to sculpt with wire with step-by-step instructions for several projects of varying complexity.

Thomas, Isabel. *Sculptures*. Milwaukee, WI: Raintree Publications, 2012.
Get started with sculpture by learning how to make all different kinds of models, techniques and styles, and examples of styles from different cultures.

PERIODICALS

E S P A C E Sculpture
4888 rue Saint-Denis
Montréal, QC H2J 2L6

Canada
(514) 844-9858
Web site: http://www.espace-sculpture.com/en.php
Canada's only sculpture magazine publishes thought-provoking articles about all kinds of contemporary sculpture. Available in English and French, the magazine endeavors to be a resource for research, knowledge, and information for everyone practicing or interested in sculpture.

Sculpture
1633 Connecticut Avenue NW, 4th floor
Washington, DC 20009
(202) 234-0555
E-mail: sculpt@dgsys.com
This magazine focuses on the art of sculpting, bringing you all different kinds of information about sculpture.

Sculpture Review
75 Varick Street, 11th Floor
New York, NY 10013
(212) 764-5645
Web site: http://www.sculpturereview.com
This publication of the National Sculpture Society is dedicated to the advancement, development, and appreciation of figurative sculpture all over the world.

APPS

Forger
Sculpt anywhere with this app by Javier Edo. Among its

features, users can enjoy 3-D navigation, use different brushes for various textures, work on multiple models at once, and more.

Sculpture! 3.0
This app by Italic Labs LC inspires sculptors and artists with color photographs of sculptures from around the world by famous photographers.

BLOGS

Kylo Chua: Eves of Eight
http://www.kylochua.asia
Follow this blog to read about the life, studies, inspirations, and creations of working sculptor Kylo Chua.

The Modern Sculpture Collector
http://www.modernsculpture.blogspot.com
Visit this blog for sculpture news, sculpture biographies, gallery and museum details, and links to more art and sculpture blogs.

MOVIES AND VIDEOS

Mark Alfrey's Sculpting with Water Clay, 2005
Mark Alfrey teaches viewers how to work with water-based clay, the tools that will come in handy, and how to work as a professional.

Sculpting Comic Book Style with John Brown, 2008
If you're into comic books, try your hand at sculpting some of your favorite characters.

CHAPTER 9

WORKING AS A JEWELER AND JEWELRY REPAIRER

Jewelers and jewelry repairers craft, repair, and sell attractive pieces of jewelry out of materials such as gold, silver, gemstones, other precious materials, stones, and beads. People have worn jewelry since the cave dwellers accessorized with bones and shells. The popularity of jewelry today shows no sign of waning.

WHAT A JEWELER AND JEWELRY REPAIRER DO

Jewelers dream up ideas for pieces. People who are interested in jewelry design and can draw well may thrive in this career. This job takes a lot of creativity and is best suited for someone with artistic abilities.

The steps taken to create jewelry are basically the same. The process begins by making a mold from a carving in wax (metal is sometimes used). The carving is set in plaster and the wax is melted out to create a cavity in the shape of the piece of jewelry. Precious metals, such

All kinds of jewelry need to be maintained, which is where the jewelry repairer comes in. Watches need their gears fixed, and rings and necklaces need stones replaced.

ON THE JOB: HANDMADE JEWELRY

Donna Sanderson is the owner of Ageratum Jewelry by Donna. She runs her business online, mainly through the craft and hand-made items site Etsy.

"I design beaded jewelry, sometimes using vintage components, lampwork, and/or dichrotic glass from other 'Etsy-ians' (or crafters), and sometimes using watch faces. Usually the colors or a special pendant bring it all together for me, and I just go with whatever feels right and makes me happy. I like that great feeling of satisfaction when I create something pretty, or even something a bit wild. That's exciting, too. There are so many beautiful designs out there, and when I see them, I can easily be inspired.

"I have always been a bit artistic and have a love and desire to do any kind of crafts. When I started beading, it was just for my own personal items. Then I guess...the jewelry just kept adding up. I gave away pieces, then sold a few, then discovered the [Etsy] site. So here I am—creating and selling.

"I have no formal training, not even an art class in grade school or high school. Although you don't need college for this line of work, it wouldn't hurt to take a few workshops to get some professional instruction on how to work with certain materials. Once you have some hands-on experience with a pro, there is no limit to your designs. Follow your heart and create what you feel."

as silver, gold, and platinum, are then melted and poured into the mold. This is what will become the metal model. When the metal is cooled, special touches may be added. The piece may need to be filed or polished before it is complete. Not all jewelry makers use molds. Some use stones, beads, and pearls to make beautiful creations.

When a piece of jewelry is broken, the jewelry repairer fixes it. He or she may replace a lost stone, resize a ring, or solder pieces together. Other days he or she may need to replace clasps or restring beads.

Jewelers who own their retail stores where they make and sell their creations have become less common. More often, jewelers work in a store owned by another person. Usually a wholesaler sells jewelry to the owner. In a retail

Jewelers use all kinds of materials to create rings, necklaces, watches, and more. They may use metals, such as silver, gold, and platinum, as well as stones, beads, and pearls.

Jewelers who are employed in retail stores often work directly with customers to help them select the jewelry they're looking for.

store, the jeweler usually works with customers, helping them find the kind of jewelry they are looking for, sometimes completing cash and credit transactions.

Design and creativity are the focal point in a jewelry designer's career. Many artists turn to jewelry making as an art form for expressing their creativity. In 1990, the American Jewelry Design Council was founded because people felt that jewelry should be considered more of an art form.

TRAINING

Community colleges and trade schools offer classes to teach jewelry making and repair. These classes are good places to learn about different precious metals and gemstones, different techniques, and computer-aided design (CAD) used to create jewelry.

Apprenticeships and on-the-job training provide hands-on experience. After two years as an apprentice, students are tested on gemstone identification, casting a mold, and engraving to become a jeweler. Finally, consider a part-time job in a jewelry store to get a feel for the atmosphere.

Art or industrial arts classes may help determine if jewelry design is worth pursuing. Industrial arts classes in particular offer experience working with machines. Jewelers use many different machines that require hand-eye coordination and good eyesight.

THE GOOD, THE BAD, AND THE UGLY

Some fields have more perks or drawbacks than others. Jewelry designers get to see their designs made into beautiful pieces of jewelry.

Anyone who decides on self-employment—like about 50 percent of jewelers—can choose his or her work environment: home or a small shop (where he or she handles customer requests). It's a personal choice.

These professions require sitting for hours while working. Jewelers must concentrate for long periods of time on the task at hand. Safety is very important in this field. Injury can easily occur if one's attention wanders. Some machines get very hot and others are sharp.

FOR MORE INFORMATION

ORGANIZATIONS

Gemological Institute of America (GIA)
World Headquarters
The Robert Mouawad Campus
5345 Armada Drive
Carlsbad, CA 92008
(800) 421-7250
Web site: http://www.gia.edu
The GIA is the world's foremost authority on diamonds, colored
   stones, and pearls. It provides resources needed to accurately and objectively determine gemstone quality. Students
   worldwide take classes and learn all about the industry.

Jewelers of America
120 Broadway, Suite 2820
New York, NY 10271
(646) 658-0246
Web site: http://www.jewelers.org
Jewelers of America is the largest trade organization for retail
   jewelers. It provides information about jewelry, such as care
   and cleaning, selecting jewelry, and choosing a jeweler.

Women's Jewelry Association (WJA)
52 Vanderbilt Avenue, 19th Floor
New York, NY 10017-3827
(212) 687-2722
Web site: http://www.womensjewelry.org
The WJA helps women in the jewelry and watch industries
   advance and develop professionally through networking,

education, leadership development, and member services.

WEB SITES

Due to the changing nature of Internet links, Rosen Publishing has developed an online list of Web sites related to the subject of this book. This site is updated regularly. Please use this link to access the list:

http://www.rosenlinks.com/CCWC/Build

BOOKS

Chin, Jennifer. *Hot Connections Jewelry: The Complete Sourcebook of Soldering Techniques.* New York, NY: Crown Publishing Group, 2011.
With this book, readers can learn basic soldering techniques and move on to more advanced techniques. It includes twenty-three lessons and fifteen projects to get started.

McGrath, Jinks. *The New Encyclopedia of Jewelry-Making Techniques.* London, England: Quarto Publishing, 2010.
This book covers all kinds of ways to start making jewelry right at home. The author provides simple step-by-step instructions and photographs of many different techniques.

PERIODICALS

Art Jewelry Magazine
Kalmbach Publishing Co.

21027 Crossroads Circle
P.O. Box 1612
Waukesha, WI 53187-1612
(800) 533-6644
Web site: http://www.art.jewelrymakingmagazines.com
Art Jewelry Magazine features projects in all kinds of
mediums, the latest news on products and tools, and
interviews from experts and artists.

Professional Jeweler
1500 Walnut Street, Suite 1200
Philadelphia, PA 19102
E-mail: askus@professionaljeweler.com
Web site: http://www.professionaljeweler.com
This magazine contains articles about news pertaining
to the jewelry industry. Go to the Web site to sign up
for a free newsletter and check statistics about jewelry.

APPS

How to Make Jewelry
This app by Beauty Linx boasts more than four hundred
videos with step-by-step instructions and tips on
making jewelry, such as necklaces, bracelets, rings,
and earrings.

Metalsmith Suite
This app by Brynmorgen Press is a useful calculation
tool for jewelers, goldsmiths, and anyone working
with precious metals. Users will find tools to do things
such as convert weights, lengths, and temperatures;

determine how much metal or wire they need for a certain project; and research hardness, history, and properties for fifty popular gemstones.

BLOGS

Beading Daily
http://www.beadingdaily.com/blogs
Beading aficionados will find plenty of information about the craft on this blog from Interweave Press, with everything from how-to basics to wire wrapping to styles like steampunk.

Jewelry Making Daily
http://www.jewelrymakingdaily.com/blogs/daily
This blog covers just about everything a jewelry maker needs. Learn about jewelry photography, business tips, metalsmithing techniques, and a whole lot more

MOVIES AND VIDEOS

Creating Wire & Beaded Jewelry, 2007
This crafts video will teach you how to use basic tools and wire to get started making your own necklaces, bracelets, and earrings.

Metalsmith Essentials: Basic Hammering and Forming, 2011
Get ready to learn about metalsmith with eight lessons to send you on your way to creating metal jewelry.

CHAPTER 10

WORKING IN THE SHOE INDUSTRY

For a long time, handmade shoes were commonplace. Shoes were only mass-produced after 1874, when Charles Goodyear invented the welt stitcher and made it possible to produce shoes by a machine. People making shoes by hand are far less common today.

Although mass production of shoes has lessened the need for cobblers, people are still needed to help construct and repair shoes. Shoe industry workers make footwear out of leather and other materials using modern machinery, such as a sanding machine. Those who like working with leather or follow current footwear styles and trends might be well suited to follow in the footsteps of other shoe industry workers.

WHAT SHOE INDUSTRY WORKERS DO

Making shoes is no simple task. One pair of shoes may be made up of 280 different parts. Shoe industry workers put these pieces together to make a pair of shoes, as well as boots, sneakers, and slippers. Because up to 150 different machine

Shoe repairers need to know how a shoe is put together and the best way to fix it. A skilled repairer can help make shoes last much longer than normal.

steps may be required, shoe industry workers must know how to use the machines.

Many different people in a factory handle each pair of shoes. An upper-leather sorter selects the right pieces of leather by quality, thickness, color, and grain. A cut-out-and-marking machine operator cuts the leather into the right size pieces and punches holes and marks where the stitching should be. Standard machine stitchers put the materials together and may stitch, glue, or staple the parts of the shoe together. Then the shoes are laced, made into different sizes, given insoles, and worked on by many other people before they're sent to the shoe store. Each employee has a very specific task.

The process of making non-leather shoes is much like leather shoe production; machines simply adjust to accommodate other materials. Manufacturing non-leather shoes is less complicated, though, because unlike leather, the fabric does not need to be inspected and more than one layer can be cut at a time.

To work with a product from start to finish, consider working as a custom shoemaker. They assemble shoes by hand or with machines, but they take care of every step. Custom shoemakers usually know about shoe repair, too. People can buy manufactured shoes easily, so having more skills can only benefit custom shoemakers and encourage customers to patronize their business.

FLUEVOG SHOES: FUNKY FEET!

John Fluevog started making wild and innovative shoes using traditional shoemaking methods in 1970. His artistic flair and attention to detail has paid off. Fast Company named Fluevog shoes one of the world's most innovative companies in the fashion industry. The Museum of Modern Art in New York featured Fluevog's stylish stompers on its calendar and a postcard. Fluevog shoes have been seen on stars like Madonna and Jack White and on the runways of high fashion.

Creative types who like designing should check out Fluevog's Open Source Footwear page on its Web site. Submit your own design ideas to the site, and if you're chosen—even if only part of the design is used—Fluevog will give you a free pair of the shoes and name the shoe after you! Check out its site regularly for contests to win free shoes, other fun Fluevog gear, and even music or concert tickets. Most contests require entrants to be creative with design. On the FluevogCreative page, footwear fans can submit their own ads. Winners don't get fame and fortune, but they do get cash, their name and bio on the site, and their art and name will be used in magazines all over the world. Obviously, it's not the way to get famous, but why not give it a try and get shoe designs out of the sketchbook and onto the street?

TRAINING

Even without knowing how shoes are made, shoe industry workers can learn how to work with the different machines from other employees. A trainee may work with another employee until he or she can do a task independently. Before becoming a custom shoemaker, however, one has to be skilled in making shoes.

Knowing how to sew and operate a sewing machine can be helpful when starting out. Some high schools offer these courses. Employers are more likely to hire employees who already have skills that are related to shoe manufacturing, such as working with machines or leather. It also helps to have good eyesight and an ability to do precise, detailed work.

Vocational schools offer classes such as shoe making and repair. Here, students learn the basic skills needed to make shoes, such as cutting, dying, and stitching leather. Some programs also teach the basics of running a small business, which can be helpful if you are interested in running your own business.

THE GOOD, THE BAD AND THE UGLY

Custom shoemakers can start their own businesses or work for a small business. By working for a small business, workers

have more flexibility to oversee production from start to finish. This might be particularly satisfying for those who like seeing a project through with tangible results.

The ability to manage the machines used in a shoe factory allows employees to cross over into work in other industries, such as clothing manufacturing and rubber goods manufacturing. These skills are valued and used in many industries, so finding a different job is considerably easier if one has experience working with machines.

Constant improvements in technology may decrease the number of jobs in shoe factories in the coming years. Machines capable of quickly handling some tasks will replace many of the tasks that are required of people.

Not everyone wants to work in a factory because it may involve working indoors and long periods of sitting. Workers must always concentrate around machines to avoid injury.

Orthopedic and therapeutic shoemakers make or modify shoes according to a doctor's recommendation. Although this profession requires additional training, the demand for orthopedic and therapeutic shoemakers is greater, especially in areas with higher populations of elderly people. And knowing that you can help someone walk easier may be all you need to consider this career.

Shoemakers who work for small or independent businesses are more apt to learn the process of making footwear from start to finish.

FOR MORE INFORMATION

ORGANIZATIONS

American Apparel & Footwear Association (AAFA)
1601 North Kent Street, Suite 1200
Arlington, VA 22209
(703) 524-1864
Web site: http://www.wewear.org
The American Apparel & Footwear Association is a national trade association that strives to promote and enhance its members' competitiveness, productivity, and profitability.

Fashion Footwear Association of New York
274 Madison Avenue, Suite 1701
New York, NY 10016
(212) 751-6422
E-mail: info@ffany.org
Web site: http://www.ffany.org
This nonprofit organization organizes footwear trade shows, which bring together people and companies to improve the footwear industry. It also sponsors charitable events and has implemented scholarship programs.

Shoe Service Institute of America
305 Huntsman Court
Bel Air, MD 21015
(410) 569-3425
E-mail: webmaster@ssia.info
The Shoe Service Institute of America seeks to further

the shoe repair industry by educating consumers about the physical, economic, and environmental benefits of purchasing and maintaining quality footwear.

WEB SITES

Due to the changing nature of Internet links, Rosen Publishing has developed an online list of Web sites related to the subject of this book. This site is updated regularly. Please use this link to access the list:

http://www.rosenlinks.com/CCWC/Build

BOOKS

Choklat, Aki. *Footwear Design*. London, England: Laurence King Publishers, 2012.
This book is a guide to getting into the design side of the shoemaking industry. It includes illustrations, tips, and tricks of the trade.

Leno, John Bedford. *The Art of Boot and Shoemaking: A Practical Handbook Including Measurement, Last-Fitting, Cutting-Out, Closing, and Making*. Seaside, OR: Rough Draft Printing, 2012.
This no-nonsense book is full of information about making shoes, including machines used in the process. It includes some illustrations and a detailed index.

PERIODICALS

American Shoemaking
Shoe Trades Publishing Company

61 Massachusetts Avenue
Arlington, MA 02174
(617) 648-8160
Web site: http://www.shoetrades.com
This bimonthly magazine focuses on educating the
reader about current footwear manufacturing news
and information. It also contains details about events
and conventions for the footwear industry.

Canadian Footwear Journal
1448 Lawrence Avenue East
North York, ON M4A 2S8
Canada
Web site: http://www.footwearjournal.com
For more than one hundred years, *Canadian Footwear
Journal* has published the latest footwear news for
retailers, manufacturers, importers, and distributors.

World Footwear Magazine
36 Crosby Road North
Liverpool L22 0QN
England
+44 (0) 151 928 9288
Web site: http://www.footwearbiz.com
In six issues a year, *World Footwear Magazine* covers
every aspect of the footwear industry: machinery,
technology, manufacturing, fashion and design, and
business management.

APPS

Upper Street Shoe Designer
Design shoes on the go with Upper Street's fantastic
new Shoe Designer app, created exclusively for the
iPad. Women everywhere can design and decorate
their own stunning luxury shoes from heel to toe. Purchase the finished shoes and wear them within weeks.

BLOGS

Bespoke Shoes Unlaced
carreducker.blogspot.com
Step into the world of two shoemakers and read about
their tools, construction methods, repairs, and more.

Chicago School of Shoemaking
http://www.chicagoschoolofshoemaking.com/blog-2
Just because someone doesn't want to attend college doesn't mean that he or she can't make use
of some resources to learn more. Check out this
blog for images and discussions about shoemaking
tools and events.

MOVIES AND VIDEOS

Basic Shoe Design and Rendering, 2009
Designers of all levels will learn the basics of what it
takes to design a basketball shoe.

CHAPTER 11

WORKING AS TAILORS AND DRESSMAKERS

Clothing has become more than a way to protect our bodies; in our society, we express our personalities with our clothes. People study clothing and fashion to make a living.

Wearing clothing started out when people needed to keep warm and survive extreme weather, but these days we choose clothing based on what styles we like. Fashion has become a major industry, and of course tailors and dressmakers are an important part of it.

WHAT TAILORS AND DRESSMAKERS DO

Typically, tailors construct men's clothing and dressmakers make women's clothing. Tailors or dressmakers sometimes work on a garment from to start to finish, but usually that only happens in smaller shops. To see a garment all the way through, consider a job in a small shop or make clothes as a hobby.

In a larger factory or store, different people are responsible for different tasks. For example, one person might sew

STITCHING TOGETHER THE SEWING MACHINE'S HISTORY

No one can deny that the invention of the sewing machine was a huge improvement over the time-consuming process of hand sewing. Machines make sewing faster, more efficient, and more precise. Working with tough materials like leather is much less frustrating. But the invention of this indispensible machine was steeped in controversy from the beginning.

Even today, there's some confusion over whom to thank for inventing the sewing machine. Elias Howe of Spencer, Massachusetts, often gets all the credit because he held patents for it in 1844. But in 1830, Bathélemy Thimonnier created the first working sewing machine in France. People were so worried that the sewing machine would mean hand stitchers would lose their jobs that Thimonnier's factory was burned down and his machines destroyed. He fled to England to escape any further harm.

Thimonnier's design was a simple machine, so in 1832–34 New York City's Walter Hunt made some improvements on it. Unfortunately for him, he never patented them. Howe did patent his own different enhancements. Howe's machine was hugely successful and copied. Eventually, a patent pool included the wildly successful Isaac Merrit Singer's design, too. More than 110,000 sewing machines were produced in 1865.

Today's machines sport computerized operations and make sewing a breeze, but the basic function remains the same. Of course, computerized sewing machines run on electricity, but the foot-powered machine is still used all over the world.

zippers into a garment or measure sleeves. Other workers have separate duties, such as measuring customers and pressing finished garments.

Tailors or dressmakers in bridal shops or large department stores must make alterations. Upscale stores usually employ a tailor or dressmaker in case a customer needs something altered.

Before any garment is created, the fabric is chosen. Fabrics come in a dizzying array of colors and textures. Next, the customer must be measured precisely. Fabric is cut to match the selected pattern. All the pieces are sewn together. The customer then goes to the tailor or dressmaker for a fitting. After areas that don't fit quite right are modified, the garment is ready to wear.

TRAINING

People who are already sewing are on the right track. The ability to sew is a necessary skill to be a tailor or dressmaker. Art classes often incorporate sewing. Or you can take a sewing class at a local recreation center.

Loving fashion is a must. Customers need help picking out clothes from the season's styles that best suit them. It's good to know about different kinds of fabric because it is the foundation of creations.

To make sure a garment fits just right, fabric must be measured and cut very carefully based on the customer's measurements and a pattern.

To jump-start a business, sew clothing and sell it to local shops or friends. An online store through a Web site like Etsy.com is another way to start out. With a customer base, one may be able to open a store and sell clothing from there.

Capable sewers can do alterations in a factory or for a large store. Through these jobs you experience working in the field and will possibly open up more career opportunities.

THE GOOD, THE BAD, AND THE UGLY

Tailor or dressmaker could be a perfect career for anyone who already loves to sew or design his or her own clothes. Sewers must be very good at their job, but passionate sewers shouldn't have trouble finding work. They get paid for what they love to do, working with

One way to get started as a tailor or dressmaker is to simply start designing and sewing clothes for friends or local shops.

like-minded people with similar interests.

Tailors and dressmakers work in textile and apparel factories, department stores, and dry cleaners. Jobs in large factories might mean dealing with a lot of noise from the machines. Most factories follow building codes to keep their workplace clean and safe.

Sewing demands time and talent, but for people who are passionate about it, this can be a satisfying career path.

FOR MORE INFORMATION

ORGANIZATIONS

American Apparel and Footwear Association (AAFA)
1601 N. Kent Street, Suite 1200
Arlington, VA 22209
(703) 524-1864
Web site: http://www.wewear.org
Founded in 2000, the AAFA represents the apparel industry by promoting education, providing news and
information, and making available resources about
the apparel industry.

Canadian Apparel Federation
151 Slater Street, Suite 708
Ottawa, ON K1P 5H3
Canada
(613) 231-3220
Web site: http://www.apparel.ca
Canadian Apparel Federation is a trade organization for
the country's apparel industry.

WEB SITES

Due to the changing nature of Internet links, Rosen Publishing has developed an online list of Web sites related
to the subject of this book. This site is updated regularly.
Please use this link to access the list:

http://www.rosenlinks.com/CCWC/Build

BOOKS

Bye, Elizabeth. *Fashion Design*. New York, NY: Berg Publishers, 2010.
Begin to think about the concept of fashion design as much more than frivolous. Readers are encouraged to think about fashion within the context of culture, economy, and ethics.

Chapin, Kari. *The Handmade Marketplace: How to Sell Your Crafts Locally, Globally, and Online*. North Adams, MA: Storey Publishing, 2010.
This book helps demystify the process of selling handmade goods like clothes. It covers everything from marketing to pricing to choosing where and how to sell.

Smith, Alison. *Dressmaking*: *The Complete Step-by-Step Guide to Making Your Own Clothes*. New York, NY: DK Adult, 2012.
Between these two covers you'll find plenty of information to get started making, altering, and customizing clothes.

PERIODICALS

Sewing Savvy
Annie's
P.O. Box 8000
Big Sandy, TX 75755
Web site: http://www.anniescatalog.com/sewing_savvy.php
Sewing enthusiasts look to this publication to get tips

on sewing, as well as informative articles, free patterns, and regular features.

Sewing World
Traplet Publications
Traplet House
Pendragon Close
Malvern WR14 1GA
England
Web site: http://www.sewingworldmagazine.com
This magazine is as much for the beginner as for the advanced stitcher. Check out projects, sewing tips and techniques, how-to tips, book reviews, show news, new product information, and feature articles on people and places involved in sewing.

Threads
The Taunton Press, Inc.
63 South Main Street
P.O. Box 5506
Newtown, CT 06470
Web site: http://www.threadsmagazine.com
Threads is a magazine for those in the garment industry. Each issue includes articles to help tailors and dressmakers learn more about their craft. Topics covered range from fabric to helpful sewing and designing tips.

APPS

iSew Academy
Choose projects to sew, and then learn from the pros

with videos and step-by-step instructions. A pattern index is regularly updated with new inspiring ideas.

Sewing Guide
This app helps users with basic but important techniques, such as installing zippers, sewing pockets, and choosing fabric.

BLOGS

Lucky Lucile
http://www.luckylucille.com
This lively blog has handy sewing (and knitting) pages, tutorials, and a fun flair for the vintage.

Trash To Couture
http://www.trashtocouture.com
Get ready to up-cycle! This blog has ideas and patterns for sewing brand-new fashions out of older clothes. A "Before and After" section is great inspiration.

MOVIES AND VIDEOS

Couture Techniques Workshop Basics, 2010
This video shows viewers that high fashion is well within reach. Learn important stitches and more that will improve your work.

Studio Sewing Skills, 2008
This video teaches sewing, fitting, designing, and draping clothing to flatter different body shapes.

CHAPTER 12

WORKING AS A DOLL MAKER

Lots of us played with dolls or action figures when we were kids. As adults, many of us are still amazed by and interested in the wide variety of dolls. There are always new dolls to collect. Dolls line the shelves of major stores, but collectors and doll appreciators everywhere seek out handmade dolls, too.

Making dolls by hand is an intricate art and involves many complicated steps. Some people enjoy making dolls as a hobby, but others take the next step and make a career out of building dolls for others to enjoy.

WHAT DOLL MAKERS DO

The duties of a doll maker depend on the kind of doll that he or she builds. All kinds of dolls are made differently, of every shape and size, and of course they are constructed with various materials. The type of doll one most likes might be a clue to the kind of dolls he or she would like to make.

Dolls can be made from something as small and simple as a corncob or string, or they can be detailed and complicated

with many kinds of materials. The popular porcelain doll is made using molds. The doll's head, or porcelain slip, is made first by pouring a mold full of liquid clay, following the manufacturer's instructions. Then the mold is put into a kiln, which is like an oven for pottery, for about eight hours.

In the kiln, the clay becomes porcelain. This porcelain head is the center around which the doll will be built. When the head is cool, the porcelain is sanded so that it is completely smooth. The features must be painted on—lips, toenails and fingernails (if the hands and feet are porcelain), and sometimes eyes. It requires some artistic ability to paint the facial features.

A wig gives the doll hair, sometimes eyelashes are added, and a body is constructed of various materials, such as cotton, bendable wire, and cloth. Beans are sometimes added to the body to give it weight. Finally, the doll is dressed. Choosing what the doll wears can be a lot of fun for those who like fashion or sewing. Cloth dolls are also very popular but require more sewing skills.

TRAINING

Anyone can begin making dolls right away. Get started with kits available at craft stores or by following a pattern online. Porcelain doll kits usually contain premade doll parts, but with more experience, some may want to learn how to make

Dolls can be made out of just about anything, with spun cotton or through a complicated process, as in the case of porcelain dolls.

One of the perks of being a doll maker is that he or she can be completely creative and make just about any kind of doll imaginable.

these parts themselves. Workshops and classes are available everywhere—more than seven hundred worldwide.

Fabric, patterns, and other materials are available at craft and fabric stores. Spare doll parts will make a first doll easier to build. Books can help get doll lovers started on almost any kind of doll making. No matter how one starts learning, remember practice makes perfect.

THE GOOD, THE BAD, AND THE UGLY

Doll makers are much like other artistic jobs. They have complete control over where they work, and they can choose their own work hours. They can choose what types of dolls they make, too, so there's lots of creative leeway.

The doll maker's salary depends on how many dolls he or she sells

CABBAGES AND RAGS

Johnny Gruelle, an illustrator and comic strip writer, originally created Raggedy Ann and Andy, who are possibly the most famous rag dolls of all time. According to the National Toy Hall of Fame, one day in 1915, Gruelle's daughter showed him her old rag doll. He drew a face on it and named her Raggedy Ann. Three years later he would write a children's book about the doll, *Raggedy Ann Stories*, and his publisher arranged to sell rag dolls with the books. By 1920, he wrote the *Raggedy Andy Stories*. In both books the dolls had lively adventures when humans weren't looking. Raggedy Ann was inducted into the National Toy Hall of Fame in 2002, and Andy joined her in 2007.

The Cabbage Patch Kid is another famous doll. Xavier Roberts started making dolls, or soft sculptures, when he came across the German technique called "needle molding." He combined this with quilting abilities that he learned from his mother. The next year, while working his way through school, Roberts came up with the idea of selling his Little People dolls with their own birth certificates.

In 1978, Roberts started delivering his dolls and birth certificates to arts and crafts shows in the southeastern United States, charging an "adoption fee." He entered and won first place in the Osceola Art Show in Kissimmee, Florida. Back at home, he and several friends fixed up an old clinic and called it "BabyLand General Hospital." Roberts's clever and creative marketing landed his unique dolls a lot of press by 1981, making it hard to keep up with demand.

and how much each doll costs. Some pick up a second job for money until they're able to live solely on what they earn as a doll maker. Some can teach a workshop on doll making or give private lessons to make extra money.

Doll makers have to work hard at making and selling their dolls. They may work weekends at crafts fairs or set up a Web site to sell them online. No matter how they decide to sell their dolls, the business side of things is almost another job in itself.

FOR MORE INFORMATION

ORGANIZATIONS

International Doll Makers Association
414 Shorewood Drive
Duncanville, TX 75116
(972) 298-7907
Web site: http://www.idmadolls.com
This site allows for doll makers to connect through clubs, workshops, competitions, and conventions. A junior membership helps get younger doll makers started.

National Institute of American Doll Artists (NIADA)
600 S. 22nd Street
Lincoln, NE 68502
E-mail: niada@niada.org
Web site: http://http://www.niada.org
The National Institute of American Doll Artists is a worldwide organization of doll artists, supportive patrons, and friends whose purpose is to promote the art of the original handmade doll. The site includes events, workshops, and tips.

Original Doll Artists Council of America
1251 Garden Circle Drive
Saint Louis, MO 63125
E-mail: info@odaca.org
Web site: http://www.odaca.org
Original Doll Artists Council of America is an international organization of artists who create original dolls and figurative sculpture. The site offers tips, events, and other resources for doll makers.

WEB SITES

Due to the changing nature of Internet links, Rosen Publishing has developed an online list of Web sites related to the subject of this book. This site is updated regularly. Please use this link to access the list:

http://www.rosenlinks.com/CCWC/Build

BOOKS

Cato, Terese. *Fanciful Cloth Dolls: From Tip of the Nose to Curly Toes*. Lafayette, CA: C&T Publishing, 2013.
Anyone handy with a needle and thread can start making their own dolls. These patterns cover everything from the basic doll to clothes and accessories.

Matthiessen, Barbara, Nancy Horner, and Rick Petersen. *The Complete Photo Guide to Doll Making*. Minneapolis, MN: Creative Publishing International, 2010.
Covering all kinds of doll making styles and techniques, this book is a great reference guide for the beginning doll maker.

PERIODICALS

Art Doll Quarterly
22992 Mill Creek Drive
Laguna Hills, CA 92653
(949) 380-7318
E-mail: customerservice@stampington.com
Web site: http://www.artdollquarterly.com
Learn all about art dolls and sculptural figures made from cloth, polymer clay, wire armatures, mixed media, and much more. The Web site includes a handy glossary and more.

Dolls Magazine
N7528 Aanstad Road
P.O. Box 5000
Iola, WI 54945-5000
(800) 753-1491
E-mail: goldiem@jonespublishing.com
Web site: http://www.dollsmagazine.com
This magazine brings a wealth of information about doll
   collecting from the top professionals in the field of
   doll making. The site includes videos, expert doll iden-
   tification, and podcasts, too.

Dolls United Interactive Magazine
Dolls United
6360 Camille Drive
Mechanicsville, VA 23111
(804) 339-8579
E-mail: editor@dollsunited.com
Web site: http://www.dollsunited.com
Dolls United Interactive Magazine is a quarterly multime-
   dia magazine for cloth art doll makers, artists, and mul-
   timedia enthusiasts. Check out a sample of the magazine on the Web site to see if you like what you see.

Soft Dolls & Animals!
Scott Publications, Inc.
2145 W. Sherman Boulevard
Muskegon, MI 49441
(231) 755-2200
Web site: http://www.scottpublications.com/sdamag
Each issue includes info for beginners and experienced
   artists who make or collect cloth dolls, teddy bears,
   or animals. Each bimonthly issue contains how-to
   projects for all, techniques on topics such as pattern

drafting and needle-sculpting, profiles on some of the world's most recognized fabric-craft artists, plus a full-size pullout pattern section.

APPS

Makies Doll Factory
Not ready to take the plunge and make a doll? With the Makies Doll Factory app by MakieLab, users can design a doll from head to toe and order an action doll to have at home. Designing the dolls is free.

BLOGS

Doll Makers Muse
dollmakersmuse.blogspot.com
This doll making blog features tips, techniques, tutorials, and inspiration about the art of whimsical doll making.

Susie McMahon Dolls
susiemcmahondolls.blogspot.com
Plenty of photos of new dolls and other knitted creations, interspersed with daily life, should keep readers inspired to create their own dolls.

MOVIES AND VIDEOS

Cloth Doll Making with Patti Medaris Culea, 2011
Go through the process of making unique cloth dolls step by step with this DVD. The video includes wiring and sculpting, dyeing the body, painting, and much more.

MD01: Porcelain Dollmaking 1, 2006
This first DVD in the series from Master Dollmakers takes beginner and advanced dollmakers through tried-and-true techniques for making dolls.

GLOSSARY

ALTERATION The act of changing.

APPRENTICESHIP The process by which a person receives instruction on how to perform a job.

COMMERCIAL BUILDING A structure that is used for business purposes.

COMMISSION Getting paid a percentage of a sale as salary.

COMMODITY Something that has a benefit, usually financial.

CONDUIT Material that is used to protect wires or cable.

DICHROTIC Showing different colors when viewed from different directions, usually referring to crystal.

FOREMAN A worker who supervises other workers.

FREELANCE A person who is paid for performing a task, but is not bound to a long-term agreement.

HYDROPONIC GARDENING A way of growing flora using nutrient solutions instead of soil.

ILLUSTRATION A drawing used to clarify something.

INSTALL The process by which something is adjusted or put into place for use.

JOURNEYMAN An experienced worker who takes on and trains an apprentice.

LIVELIHOOD The occupation by which a person is financially supported.

MACHINIST A person skilled in operating machines or machine tools.

MAINTENANCE Upkeep to ensure that something is kept in proper condition.

PATENT A governmental grant that is given to an inventor, granting the person the sole right to use the product for profit.

PESTICIDE A chemical used to kill insects and other pests.

PHOTOSYNTHESIS The process by which plants use carbon dioxide, water, and sunlight to produce carbohydrates and oxygen.

RESIDENTIAL BUILDING A structure used for living purposes.

SOLDERED Joined together with metal.

STAMINA The ability to withstand long periods of mental or physical fatigue; endurance.

TECHNOLOGY The application of science to industry or commerce.

THREE-DIMENSIONAL Having the appearance of length, depth, and breadth.

TRADE An occupation that requires skilled labor.

UNION An organized group of workers who get together to protect and further their rights and interests.

VARIATION The extent toward which something can be different; change.

WHOLESALER One who sells goods in large quantities.

INDEX

ABOUT THE AUTHOR

Heather Moore Niver has written more than twenty nonfiction children's books on a variety of subjects, including careers. She lives, writes, and raises sheep in New York State with her husband and stepdaughter.

PHOTO CREDITS

Cover, p. 3 © iStockphoto.com/Andrejs Pidjass; pp. 7, 46 Wavebreakmedia Ltd./the Agency Collection/Getty Images; p. 10 © Peter Fürster/picture-alliance/dpa/AP Images; p. 12 Hemera/Thinkstock; p. 21 michaejung/Shutterstock.com; p. 23 runzelkorn/Shutterstock.com; pp. 25, 56 kurhan/Shutterstock.com; p. 31 Digital Vision/Thinkstock; p. 32 Bart Coenders/E+/Getty Images; p. 36 Blend Images/Shutterstock.com; pp. 42–43 Stephen Coburn/Shutterstock.com; p. 54 Comstock/Thinkstock; p. 63 altrendo images/Stockbyte/Getty Images; p. 66 iStockphoto/Thinkstock; p. 73 Glow Images, Inc./Getty Images; pp. 76–77 Simon Battensby/Photographer's Choice/Getty Images; pp. 84–85 Steve Williams Photo/Workbook Stock/Getty Images; p. 88 Mary Bingham/Shutterstock.com; p. 95 altrendo images/Getty Images; p. 97 Walter Bibikow/age fotostock/Getty Images; pp. 98–99 poba/E+/Getty Images; p. 106 Fuse/Thinkstock; p. 110 istockphoto/Thinkstock; p. 119 Diego Cervo/Shutterstock.com; pp. 120–121 Image Source/Getty Images; p. 122 Asiaselects/Getty Images; p. 128 John Burke/Photolibrary/Getty Images; pp. 130–131 Amy Kozlova/Flickr/Getty Images; cover and interior design elements © iStockphoto.com/pialhovik (banner), © iStockphoto.com/David Shultz (dots), Melamory/Shutterstock.com (hexagon pattern), Lost & Taken (boxed text background texture), biorave/Shutterstock.com (chapter opener pages icons)

Designer: Brian Garvey; Editor: Nicholas Croce;
Photo Researcher: Marty Levick